EVENTS THAT CHANGED THE COURSE OF HISTORY:

THE STORY OF THE ATTACK ON PEARL HARBOR 75 YEARS LATER

Kimberly Sarmiento

EVENTS THAT CHANGED THE COURSE OF HISTORY: THE STORY OF THE ATTACK ON PEARL HARBOR 75 YEARS LATER

Copyright © 2016 Atlantic Publishing Group, Inc.

1405 SW 6th Avenue • Ocala, Florida 34471 • Phone 800-814-1132 • Fax 352-622-1875
Web site: www.atlantic-pub.com • E-mail: sales@atlantic-pub.com
SAN Number: 268-1250

Library of Congress Cataloging-in-Publication Data

Names: Sarmiento, Kimberly, 1975- author.
Title: Events that changed the course of history : the story of the attack on
    Pearl Harbor 75 years later / by Kimberly Sarmiento.
Description: Ocala, Florida : Atlantic Publishing Group, Inc., 2016. |
    Includes bibliographical references and index. | Audience: Grade 9 to 12.
Identifiers: LCCN 2016019606 (print) | LCCN 2016025829 (ebook) | ISBN
    9781620231425 (alk. paper) | ISBN 1620231425 (alk. paper) | ISBN
    9781620231494 ()
Subjects: LCSH: Pearl Harbor (Hawaii), Attack on, 1941.
Classification: LCC D767.92 .S346 2916 (print) | LCC D767.92 (ebook) | DDC
    940.54/26693--dc23
LC record available at https://lccn.loc.gov/2016019606

Printed in the United States

PROJECT MANAGER: Rebekah Sack • rsack@atlantic-pub.com
ASSISTANT EDITOR: Rebekah Sack • rsack@atlantic-pub.com
INTERIOR LAYOUT: Steven W. Booth • steven@geniusbookcompany.com
COVER DESIGN: Jackie Miller • sullmill@charter.net
JACKET DESIGN: Steven W. Booth • steven@geniusbookcompany.com

Reduce. Reuse. RECYCLE.

A decade ago, Atlantic Publishing signed the Green Press Initiative. These guidelines promote environmentally friendly practices, such as using recycled stock and vegetable-based inks, avoiding waste, choosing energy-efficient resources, and promoting a no-pulping policy. We now use 100-percent recycled stock on all our books. The results: in one year, switching to post-consumer recycled stock saved 24 mature trees, 5,000 gallons of water, the equivalent of the total energy used for one home in a year, and the equivalent of the greenhouse gases from one car driven for a year.

Over the years, we have adopted a number of dogs from rescues and shelters. First there was Bear and after he passed, Ginger and Scout. Now, we have Kira, another rescue. They have brought immense joy and love not just into our lives, but into the lives of all who met them.

We want you to know a portion of the profits of this book will be donated in Bear, Ginger and Scout's memory to local animal shelters, parks, conservation organizations, and other individuals and nonprofit organizations in need of assistance.

– Douglas & Sherri Brown,
President & Vice-President of Atlantic Publishing

For my grandmother who lost her older brother in the war;
and to all those who fell at Pearl Harbor, may time never forget you.

TABLE OF CONTENTS

INTRODUCTION

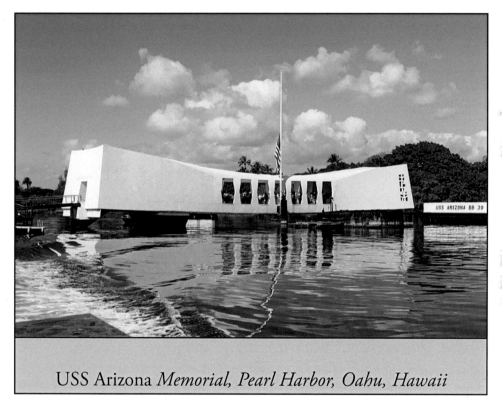

USS Arizona *Memorial, Pearl Harbor, Oahu, Hawaii*

For those of you born at the dawn of the 21st Century, thoughts of driving tests, whether or not to attend prom, and perhaps even college applications are dancing through your heads. Unless you have a history test pending, World War II probably doesn't register too high on your radar. Maybe you heard a lecture about Pearl Harbor last December. Who can be sure? At that time of year, you're focused on semester exams, winter holidays, and finally getting some time off of school.

To you, Pearl Harbor might be that Ben Affleck and Josh Hartnett movie your teacher played you. Even that movie is as old as you are now, so how are you supposed to connect to things that happened so long ago? Sure, December 7th is the "day that will live in infamy," but what does infamy even mean?

This book is dedicated to helping you connect to that day and will hopefully help you come to care about it. An 18-year-old sailor who survived the attack at Pearl Harbor would be turning 93 this year — someone you probably think you have little in common with. However, all those years ago, that teenage sailor would have been thinking about the same things you do every December 7th — holidays, seeing family, and perhaps even dancing with a love interest to festive music.

As you inch closer to high school graduation, you will be thinking a lot about what comes next. For you or some of your friends, joining the military might seem like a good option, because you can earn money for college and see the world. The young sailors, aircrew, and nurses stationed in Hawaii back then probably thought the same thing. In fact, they were likely thrilled to find themselves in such a beautiful island paradise.

That all changed the morning of December 7th, 1941. Not only was paradise ruined, at least temporarily, but the U.S. was now in a war that would change everything. Before the war, Americans wanted to focus on our country; after, our leaders wanted to help rebuild all the places that were damaged during the fighting. It was a good thing to do, but it also made us more important to the world than we had ever been.

A scenic overview of Pearl Harbor. The USS Arizona *Memorial can be seen just above the battleship.*

Another thing that changed was how nervous we made other countries. We had made and used the world's first Atomic bomb, and the Soviet Union wasn't too happy about it. They wanted to know our secrets, so they sent spies to figure it out. By 1949, they had tested their own Atomic bomb. What followed was a "Cold War" where the two countries "fought" without actually physically fighting each other. You've probably seen some of your friends fight like this, so you know that not much gets resolved, and it seems to last forever.

Good things followed World War II as well. The U.S. economy grew by leaps and bounds, and the American people were generally better off than they had been beforehand. Also, there were huge technological gains during the war. The world's first computers were developed to help the military break code, and Motorola became a major research and development company, eventually leading to the world's first cell phones.

So, while a teenaged sailor swabbing the deck of a battleship back in 1941 wouldn't have been able to snap a shot of the Japanese Zeros that flew overhead from his iPhone, it's his legacy that lets you do that today.

Learning to drive is one of the biggest milestones in any teenager's life. Studying the rules of the road for your written exam, practicing the maneuvers you will be tested on, remembering to check your mirrors instead of playing with the radio as your mom or dad glares at you from the passenger's seat — it's all part of the process. Then, you get your driver's license and feel like you have accomplished something big. You have, but you have also taken on big responsibilities, and if you can't remember all those rules you studied, cops will be there to remind you with a ticket.

Studying history is kind of like remembering all the rules of driving. If we forget what has already happened and how we got where we are today, there can be consequences. History is really quite complicated — policies and decisions of yesterday are constantly impacting our lives today. Occurrences at the beginning are still influencing decisions 75 years down the line. So, we study history like the attack at Pearl Harbor to try to figure out what we can learn from it.

One thing we can learn is how not to blame the wrong people when something bad happens. After Pearl Harbor, people hated the Japanese — even the innocent Japanese-Americans. That hatred lasted a long time after the war but is mostly gone today. We've seen something similar happen much more recently.

If you think back to 9/11, Americans had that same kind of attitude toward Muslims, and it still hasn't faded completely. In fact, for those of you who will be old enough to vote soon, you will probably hear that attitude in politics a little while longer. Looking at what we got wrong before might help you figure out which of our leaders has the right attitude now.

We also need to remember Pearl Harbor because the people who were actually in it won't be here to tell their stories much longer. Only about 2,000 survivors of Pearl Harbor are thought to still be alive. In 2014, former Louisiana state Senator Jackson B. Davis was interviewed by the Washington Post. Davis had gotten used to talking to various groups about his experience as a Navy officer and survivor of Pearl Harbor. That year, he said no one had reached out to him.

"It's the same old story," Davis said. "We don't hear much about Gettysburg anymore, or Bunker Hill. Or when the Normans took over England — we don't hear much about that." Davis was

95 that year and resigned to become a part of history (Holley 2014). He might have accepted that most people don't care that much about days that live so vividly in his mind, but we should not be so ready to let go. We should still strive to care, honor, and remember.

After all, if you were on that ship and had your teenage daydreams interrupted by explosions, wouldn't you want to be remembered? We honor those who fought and died that day by making them more than just a standardized test question.

We honor them by remembering the "day that will live in infamy."

The battleship Missouri in Pearl Harbor, Hawaii. The ship now serves as a memorial and museum.

CHAPTER 1:
PEARL HARBOR BEFORE THE WAR

A view of Honolulu city, Oahu, Hawaii.

When you think of Hawaii, you could imagine anything from pristine beaches and luaus to surfing and scuba diving. Even with the *USS Arizona* Memorial in Honolulu, it's easy to forget that island paradise was once the site of a major bombing.

Fast Fact: Hawaii (Maui, specifically) ranks 7th on the U.S. News & World Report's "World's Best Places to Visit" list.

The island of Oahu has changed a lot since 1941. Less than 450,000 people lived in Hawaii then. Hawaii wasn't even a state when the bombing of Pearl Harbor occurred. Until August of 1959, Hawaii was a U.S. territory like Puerto Rico is today. The islands were still considered important for protecting our West Coast. For that reason, many members of the U.S. Navy found themselves stationed at one of the most beautiful places in the Pacific.

The Natural Pearl Harbor

Pearl Harbor was originally an extensive shallow embayment called Wai Moni (meaning Waters of Pearl) by the Hawaiians. Legend states that it was the home of a shark goddess named Ka'ahupahau and her brother Kahi'uka. Originally, the harbor was not a good fit for boats to dock. In 1778, when British seafarer Captain James Cook visited the islands, he found a coral reef barred the entrance of the location. For that reason, he decided it would be better to dock his ship at Honolulu Harbor instead (**www.nps.gov**).

Many years later, when the U.S. Navy began exploring the Hawaiian Islands, a naval officer concluded that Pearl Harbor was viable if you removed the obstructing reef. This idea was not put into motion at the time because the U.S. had no rights to Pearl Harbor. However, 35 years later, the Reciprocity Treaty between the U.S. and Hawaiian Kingdom gave Pearl Harbor to the U.S. in exchange for letting Hawaiian sugar enter the country duty-free. America could then develop Pearl Harbor if it wanted to, but it was left alone until after the start of the 20th Century.

What changed? The answer is the Spanish-American War. When Manila was captured during that war, U.S. leaders decided they needed a base in the Pacific to maintain control of the Philippines. To meet that need, it looked to Hawaii. In 1902, the entry channel in front of Pearl Harbor was dredged, deepened, and widened to create a larger opening. Over time, the passage was expanded to 600 feet wide and 35 feet deep, allowing a full range of vessels access to the harbor, from battleships to massive aircraft carriers (**www.nps.gov**).

In 1908, Congress authorized the creation of a naval base at Pearl Harbor. By 1914, the Marines and the Army had bases there, too. The U.S. military spent two decades expanding the Navy's presence in the Pacific. It opened two airfields nearby to house the airplanes and bombers used on their aircraft carriers. When tensions between Japan and the U.S. increased in the late 1930s, the U.S. Navy created a Pacific Fleet to be stationed at Pearl Harbor full-time (Fischer 2015).

The Naval Presence at Pearl Harbor

As America began to stretch from "sea to shining sea," it became obvious that a Navy based only on the East Coast couldn't defend every part of the country. It was only natural that the Navy would eventually be split into at least two fleets. The Navy tried a couple of different formations before it settled on three fleets: the Atlantic, Pacific, and Asiatic. Up until 1940, the operation that would become the Pacific Fleet was stationed along the West Coast, primarily in San Diego, California. In response to Japanese expansion, the Navy moved that fleet to Pearl Harbor in early 1941.

As you study world history, you may have noticed how important a superior navy has been to countries with "great empires." Greece, Persia, China, Great Britain, Spain, and France under Napoleon are all given credit as strong naval powers. That was the case in World War I. Post-war talks of disarmament focused on the volume of naval warships each country could possess. No one really understood how important airplanes and air battle were going to become.

Japanese WWII torpedo bomber on an aircraft carrier.

As a result, when Japan wanted to weaken the U.S. in the Pacific, it focused primarily on America's Navy, which was pretty big. In 1941, the U.S. Navy ranged from small submarines to large battleships. There were more ships than you can probably imagine at Pearl Harbor the morning of the bombing. Some of the ships were completely sunk, but many others had only minor damage (or no damage at all).

Have you ever played battleship? You may have noticed the different shapes and sizes of the ships. To help us wrap our heads around what kind of ships were involved, let's look through some definitions from **ww2ships.com**:

- **Aircraft Carriers:** This ship is designed to carry aircraft. This kind of carrier allows aircraft to launch and land.

- **Battleships:** You probably can guess what this kind of ship is for. A capitol ship (which is basically a ship that exceeds 10,000 tons or is equipped with a gun larger than eight inches in caliber) is intended to fight other ships at sea. It's well armed, heavily armored, and it moves pretty slowly.

- **Cruisers:** This ship is somewhat smaller than a battleship, and the gun on this one is larger than five inches in caliber. Cruisers were usually armed with torpedo tubes and were generally built for speed.

- **Destroyers:** These ships are also a give-away based on the name. This vessel was typically fitted with four to six main guns, smaller caliber canons or machineguns, torpedoes, mine sweeping equipment, depth charges, and sonar. In case you aren't sure what a depth charge is, it's a weapon that's used to destroy submarines. This ship is even smaller than a cruiser with guns smaller than 5.1 inches in caliber.

- **Submarines:** Any vessels of war designed to submerge below the surface of the water.

On December 7th, 1941, the U.S. Navy had a lot of ships at Pearl Harbor, but probably not as many as Japan hoped. The list included:

- 8 out of 17 total battleships

- 2 out of 18 heavy cruisers (another 8 were on missions at sea)

- 6 out of 19 light cruisers

- 29 out of 171 total destroyers

- 4 out of 112 submarines

- Several minesweepers and minelayers

(**www.history.navy.mil** and **www.navsource.org**)

While the Navy's presence at Pearl Harbor was significant, we wonder if enough ships were actually docked there to achieve Japanese goals. The most serious damage was done to the battleships, but some were repaired and were able to participate in the war again before it was over.

Fast Fact: The aircraft carriers that would have been at the harbor that day were out at sea (along with several cruisers). Their return was delayed due to stormy weather.

Also, changes in how we fought war — and the importance of air combat — proved that taking out the battleships wasn't that big of a deal. As it turns out, the aircraft carriers that were absent that day were key to the U.S. winning the war.

The "Impenetrable" Pearl Harbor

As we study the attack on Pearl Harbor, one of the questions we have to ask is whether or not it could have been prevented. To answer that question, we have to look at one of the things that made Pearl Harbor so special. It kind of comes down to what they say is so important about all real estate — *location, location, location!*

See, the Japanese thought that if they could hit the American fleet in Hawaii, the U.S. would pull out of the region. That would have made it a lot easier for Japan to keep conquering countries in the Pacific. Well, as it turns out, the Japanese were wrong about our reaction, but the U.S. got something very wrong, too. They thought Pearl Harbor was "impenetrable."

Right now, you might be thinking "*They thought what? Why?*" The answer comes down to nature. You could only get to the naval station through narrow waterways that were only 40 feet deep. They were fully protected by anti-submarine nets. The waters were also so shallow that normal torpedoes were useless. The Navy really thought the harbor was defended well by Mother Nature.

Of course, the Japanese just changed their torpedoes and attacked from the air, but what do they say about hindsight? It's

20/20. Unfortunately, the Navy thought it was so safe that the fleet was lined up in what they called "Battleship Row." When Japanese Zeros flew overhead, this was an easy target for their pilots (**www.historylearningsite.co.uk**).

When an attack like this happens, people really want to know whose fault it is. It didn't take long for blame to be assigned and people to get in trouble, but in the years that followed, historians really started to wonder if this was a mistake that could have been avoided. One reason this question persists is because of someone who had an inkling way before 1941. His name was Billy Mitchell.

Fast Fact: Billy Mitchell is sometimes called the "Father of the U.S. Air Force."

William (Billy) Mitchell was a U.S. Army general who served in France during World War I. He later commanded all American air combat units in that country. Before anyone else imagined that airplanes would someday be more important than naval ships, he argued that bombers could sink battleships. This is something he eventually proved — even though he had to break a few rules to do so.

Mitchell wanted the U.S. to create an independent Air Force equal to the Army and Navy. He didn't win much support, but eventually, the U.S. Air Force was formed on September 18, 1947. However, as early as 1921, Mitchell said a large number of bombers could be built at the same price as one battleship (and could sink that battleship). So, it didn't make sense to keep making battleships when you should be building bombers.

To prove it, Mitchell got permission to perform bombing tests on captured German navy ships. The Navy set restrictions that Mitchell didn't like (because they wouldn't exist in war). He ignored their rules, and his airmen dropped six 2,000-pound bombs on the *Ostfriesland,* sending it to the bottom of the ocean (**http://blog.nasm.si.edu**).

Even though the conditions of the test were not exactly "war like" like Mitchell wanted, they were eerily similar to the situation U.S. battleships were in on December 7th, 1941 — anchored and unable to maneuver. Mitchell had proven that air power could sink a ship 20 years before Pearl Harbor, but that was not the end of his warnings.

General Billy Mitchell, the controversial advocate for military aviation, standing beside a pursuit plane; 1922.

In 1924, Mitchell went on an inspection tour in Hawaii and Asia. He created a 300+ page report that predicted a future war with Japan and a possible attack on Pearl Harbor (Melinger 1997). Why didn't the Navy listen to him? Well, it probably thought he was crazy or paranoid and had no idea that he would turn out to be right. After all, it had a lot of reasons to think he was wrong.

One of the biggest reasons goes back to this notion that Pearl Harbor was "impenetrable." Remember that normal torpedoes wouldn't have done much damage, because the Japanese had to alter them. See, if they had used average torpedoes, the weapons would've just dived in and stuck right to the bottom of the ocean floor. Our leaders underestimated how ingenious the Japanese could be, and it cost us big time.

Months before the attack, their designers created finned torpedoes that could perform a "feat like that of an acrobat high-diving in shallow water." By late 1941, they had the perfect weapon to use against the U.S. Navy and no "natural defense" was going to stop it (Placide 2012).

The Japanese in Hawaii Prior to WWII

When the Japanese bombed Pearl Harbor in 1941, it turns out that they were also attacking a lot of people who may have been their distant relatives. Japanese people had been living in Hawaii for decades by then, and they made up a large portion of the population.

They started moving to Hawaii in the mid-1800s when they went to work for American businessmen as farm workers. The first immigrants had been cooks, brewers, potters, printers, tailors, wood workers, and hairdressers. Needless to say, they weren't really ready for the hard labor that the plantation required.

Fast Fact: 37% of Hawaii's population was of Japanese ethnicity.

Later on, some of them said their employers were cruel and didn't stick to the work agreement. However, some Japanese went to work in California on a different kind of farm. When that didn't work out, some of them stayed in Hawaii and California (**www. everyculture.com**).

Even if the first Japanese in America and Hawaii were disappointed (or even mad) about how things turned out, that didn't stop others from trying. In 1886, Hawaii and Japan made an agreement that brought over a large number of Japanese workers, and many student workers went to California. Japanese immigration was met with mixed feelings, and some people treated them very poorly. Things got so tense that in 1906, a San Francisco school board made Japanese-American students go to a school for the Chinese.

The general attitude toward the Japanese in America was not making the Japanese government very happy. That concerned President Theodore Roosevelt who wanted a positive relationship with Japan. He said the anti-Japanese actions in California were unacceptable, and he wanted to make Japanese immigrants U.S. citizens.

The President convinced California lawmakers to be more accepting of Japanese students, but he also had to limit immigration to make sure things didn't get worse. The result was a "Gentlemen's Agreement" that allowed Japanese who had already been to the U.S. to return and for Japanese working in the U.S. to bring over their family members. Other than that, no new Japanese would come into America.

Japanese schoolchildren.
Photo Credit: javarman / Shutterstock.com

Unlike other Asian immigrants, Japanese men really wanted to marry Japanese women. To do so, they sometimes had to ask their parents for help. Many Japanese women came to Hawaii and the U.S. as "picture brides." Basically, their parents set up the marriage, and they gave the couple some pictures so that they could find each other when the woman arrived (**www. everyculture.com**).

That probably sounds pretty strange to you. How would they know if they liked each other? What if they didn't find each other attractive? What if either of them turned out to be a jerk?

Those are all important questions to ask, but back then, they were ignored. It was more important to them that they marry Japanese than that they marry for love. That way of looking at things started to disintegrate, however, as time went on.

Things continued this way for several years until 1924. President Calvin Coolidge signed an Immigration Act that placed a ban on all Japanese immigration. The act put a limit on immigration from a lot of other countries as well. By then, it really didn't matter — the Japanese were already the largest percentage of Hawaii's population. A whole generation of Hawaii-born Japanese (which means they were U.S. citizens) had been born and were growing up thinking of themselves as Americans. This second generation of Japanese was different in the following ways (**www.loc.gov**):

- They spoke English fluently.

- They were more likely to be Christians than Buddhists.

- They generally preferred "American" food, sports, and music instead of traditions from Japan.

When the bombs fell on Pearl Harbor, there were 160,000 people living in Hawaii with a Japanese background. Because people became very afraid of the Japanese during World War II, difficult times were ahead for those Hawaiians. Things didn't get as bad for them as it did for Japanese-Americans on the mainland. Eventually, they were allowed to serve in the U.S. military, and they did so with valor (courage).

However, for a while, they were kind of like a people without a homeland.

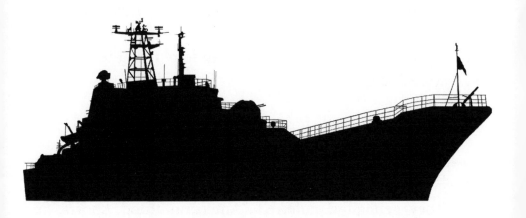

CHAPTER 2: WHY DID THE JAPANESE ATTACK?

Many Japanese were living in Hawaii, and President Franklin Roosevelt wanted to have good relations with them. That leads us to the big question: why did Japan attack Pearl Harbor?

The answer is complicated, and we may have prevented it if we had done things differently. You might not know this, but not all historians agree on the date that WWII began. For the U.S., it's simple — December 7th, 1941. However, the events that led to Pearl Harbor actually began many years before in China.

 *Fast Fact:* The attack on Pearl Harbor really started 12 days earlier "when five boats from the Japanese forces launched on November 25" (**http://interesting-facts.com**).

Even though some historians say that World War II began when Germany invaded Poland in 1939, others say it began two years earlier when Japan invaded China from Manchuria. Either way, the war was going on for several years before the U.S. got involved. Some wonder that if Japan hadn't bombed Pearl Harbor, maybe the U.S. never would've officially joined the war.

In that way, Japan attacking Pearl Harbor seems like a huge mistake. Why involve the U.S. in the war for no reason? To understand why the Japanese attacked, we have to look at a lot of different things, including political ideologies, economic factors, and what Japan actually hoped to achieve.

Political Ideologies

In the years between World War I and World War II, people in countries like Germany, Italy, and Japan developed feelings that you may not understand today. Sure, we talk about patriotism, and we still pledge allegiance to the flag, but we aren't looking to conquer other countries and make them part of the U.S.

A WWI cemetery.

That's the kind of thing Napoleon and Alexander the Great did. People don't really think like that anymore, right? In the 1930s, some people still did. Hitler wanted to expand Germany's borders in Europe, and Mussolini wanted to take over part of Africa. What did the Japanese want? They wanted to be the No. 1 country in all of Asia.

Some historians think that world leaders punished Germany too much at the end of World War I. They think Germany just wanted to conquer other countries to end financial suffering in the 1930s. Well, the Great Depression didn't just hurt America. It hurt a lot of other countries.

Germany wasn't alone in having a bad economy. Besides, what Germany did to the Jews and other minorities during the Holocaust had nothing to do with restoring prosperity. That's why other historians think it was really the rise of Nazism in Germany and fascism in Italy (and the overthrow of their governments) that led to the war.

Neither Nazism nor fascism really survived World War II. As a system of government, Nazism and fascism had very short life spans. That might lead you to ask why they came about at all. The answer might surprise you.

In fact, it kind of explains why other countries in Europe didn't mess with them at first. You see, they came about as a response to communism. Are you confused now? That's understandable. From the way America feels about these types of governments, you probably think they are all kind of the same thing, but they really aren't.

First, Nazism and fascism are really similar. They were basically totalitarian systems that said the government owned everything and the individual had no rights. This type of government was very different than governments in places like the U.S. and the UK who have laws to protect individual and property rights. However, it was also very different from communism.

In the early 1900s, the Bolshevik Revolution in Russia overthrew the last Czars and eventually led to the establishment of a communist state. This was a government system that was based on Karl Marx's "Communist Manifesto" (written in 1848). It promotes a classless society with common ownership of all land. Its number one rule is to take "from each according to his ability" and give "to each according to his needs" (**www. businessdictionary.com**).

Thousands of years ago, people lived in small tribes, and the hunters would bring back food that everyone would eat — this is essentially communism. The idea is that there should be no rich people with more than they need and no poor people living without. In a lot of ways, that may sound good. However, capitalists really didn't like it.

If you are confused about why communism sounded so horrible, try this exercise: How do you think you would feel if your entire social class was graded in a communistic style? Each student would contribute points (grades) according to his or her capabilities. Then, every student would take points (grades) according to his or her needs. Then you're stuck with the confusing question of how you define need.

Who has the greater need: the student who needs to avoid failing, the student who needs to stay on the football team, or the student trying to earn a scholarship to college? In the end, if people don't feel like they are being treated fairly, they lose motivation to work hard. That means one thing — everybody loses together.

That does not mean that all communist governments are failures. After WWII, China became a communist country and remains so to this day. China has a thriving economy, but a very different way of life and culture than we do in the U.S.

 *Fast Fact:* The only communist countries left in the world today are China, Cuba, Laos, North Korea, and Vietnam.

Perhaps capitalists really didn't need to worry about the spread of communism after all — but they did. While the U.S. didn't like Nazism or fascism, they also weren't sure if they should be allies with the Soviet Union. That wasn't the only thing that kept America out of the war.

While other countries were looking to expand their borders, the U.S. had developed a sense of "isolationism." Simply put, the American people just didn't want to get involved in other people's wars or affairs.

American Isolationism (as it was known) came about partly because of how many people died in World War I. People couldn't understand why our soldiers died in a war that didn't affect us. The financial devastation of the Great Depression didn't help things either. People didn't think we could afford to go to war. When WWII started, the general public opinion in America was to "**stay out of it.**"

With all the movies you've probably seen about WWI and WWII, you may think the country was full of people who proudly served in wars that "saved the world." It's true that the people who fought in those wars were very brave. It's just that people didn't understand how important it all was at the time. Senator Gerald P. Nye, a Republican from North Dakota, claimed that American bankers and arms manufacturers had pushed for U.S. involvement in WWI for their own profit (**https://history. state.gov**).

In light of this attitude, the U.S. Congress rejected membership in the League of Nations. In 1931, President Herbert Hoover passed the Stimson Doctrine (named after his Secretary of State, Henry Stimson), which stated that the U.S. would not recognize territory gained by aggression. However, the policy did not promise to help any country that was attacked. This is why the U.S. kind of cut things off with Japan when they attacked China, but didn't really help out either.

When Franklin D. Roosevelt became president, he wanted to change things, but he found that hard to do. He believed that the U.S. needed to take more action, but he also knew neither Congress nor the American people agreed. Even as Italy and Germany took over other countries, the U.S. Congress pushed through a series of Neutrality Acts, which prevented American ships and citizens from becoming entangled in outside conflicts. When full scale war broke out in 1939, popular opinion only shifted from favoring complete neutrality to supporting limited U.S. aid to the Allies. (**https://history.state.gov**).

The result of U.S. non-involvement in the early years of World War II was that by mid-1941, things were pretty bad for our allies. Their cities were getting destroyed by bombs, they were running low on supplies, and they were losing the war. Roosevelt got the U.S. Land Lease Act passed in March of 1941, allowing the U.S. to provide material support, but that was about it.

Fire fighting during WWII Battle of Britain. Firemen at work in a bomb-damaged street in London; 1941.

When the Germans invaded the Soviet Union in June of that same year, American and British leaders thought they would fall to the Nazis quickly. They didn't, but it cost them a lot to not lose. On the Pacific front, Japan was busy expanding and disrupting trade routes.

President Roosevelt and Prime Minister Winston Churchill met in August of 1941 to figure out how the U.S. could help. Both Roosevelt and Churchill were hoping for direct U.S. involvement in the war, but neither man got what he wanted until the Japanese attacked Pearl Harbor just a few months later.

Growing Tensions With Japan

The previous section covered the differences in political ideologies that led to WWII, but Japan was still ruled by an Emperor back then. Perhaps Imperial Japan wasn't all that different than the British or Spanish empires that first colonized America. However, Japan wasn't looking to conquer "natives" — Japan was trying to take territory away from established countries. Since it didn't work out that well, you might wonder why Japan did it to begin with.

The first reason has to do with changes in Japan's economy. Japan is a small island in the Pacific without a lot of natural resources. As it began to industrialize, the Japanese quickly learned that the resources they did have were not the right ones to support their economy. Japan came to rely heavily on imported materials like these:

- Coal

- Iron

- Steel

- Tin

- Copper

- Petroleum

While Japan was building up its trade relationships, it also built a strong military industrial complex that supported a powerful army and navy (Higgs 2006).

Eventually, Japan came to believe that the need to expand beyond its natural borders was a matter of national security. Japan had plantations in colonial territories such as Taiwan, Korea, and Manchuria, that yielded important goods for the commercial side of Japan's economy. At the height of its pre-WWII empire, Japan's territory stretched from mainland China to Micronesia. The Japanese felt they needed to protect that territory with a strong navy (**http://classroom.synonym.com**).

Much earlier in history, America and several European countries went through periods that could be viewed as imperialistic. In the 1930s, the U.S. stretched from "sea to shining sea," and the British Commonwealth was made up of the following countries:

- India

- Australia

- Canada

- South Africa

- New Zealand

- Ireland (Note: Ireland was neutral during WWII.)

It doesn't seem like the U.S. or the UK would oppose Japanese expansion on "moral" grounds. What were they going to say? "It was fine when we did it, but *you* can't." Still, they did criticize

Japan's ambitions and made attempts to stop their military from growing.

When Emperor Hirohito started his rule in 1926, Japan was becoming as nationalistic as Germany and Italy. It was also growing in industrialization and military strength. However, it was clear that Western powers didn't like the idea of Japan growing. When five major naval superpowers (the U.S., Great Britain, France, Italy, and Japan) met at the Washington Naval Conference in 1921 and 1922, the world was looking for a way to prevent another war. Japan's growing military strength worried other world leaders. Japan was a very different culture, and the other world leaders didn't understand or trust it.

No one wanted to upset the Japanese. The countries talked about having everyone disarm or make fewer warships. In the treaty that was signed, the **Five-Power Treaty**, the five countries attending the conference decided to limit the amount of warship tons (or weight) that each country could build.

Since different ships had more or less tonnage, each country got to decide which types of ships they would focus on. The U.S. and the UK were allowed to keep bigger navies, since they needed ships in both the Atlantic and Pacific Oceans. Japan was allowed a slightly smaller amount with France and Italy being allowed the least.

The U.S., the UK, France, and Japan signed the **Four-Power Treaty**. It said that each country would consult with each other before taking action in future conflicts in Asia. Clearly, neither treaty did much to prevent WWII.

There was still one more agreement that came out of the Washington Naval Conference. It was called the **Nine-Power Treaty**, and the following countries signed it:

- The U.S.

- The UK

- Japan

- France

- Italy

- Belgium

- Netherlands

- Portugal

- China

This treaty said that each country agreed to respect China. It gave Manchuria to Japan, but otherwise protected China and each country's right to do business with them (**https://history. state.gov**).

Despite the efforts of those "peace" treaties, the U.S. government still passed the Immigration Act of 1924, which banned all immigration from Asian countries. It also set limits on immigrants from other countries. Japan was not specifically targeted, but it still didn't sit well with Japanese leaders.

Like many other countries, Japan suffered during the Great Depression in America. It faced price hikes, unemployment, falling exports, and social unrest. By the 1930s, the Japanese decided they needed to improve things by force.

 *Fast Fact:* The Great Depression in America caused Germany's unemployment rate to be 25 percent by 1932 (six million people without jobs).

Unemployed men queued outside a soup kitchen in Chicago during the Great Depression.

In September of 1931, the Japanese army moved further into Manchuria and set up the state of Manchukuo. Afterward, Japanese delegates walked out of the League of Nations when the League supported China. Over the next several years, Japan designed a plan to unite Asia against the West under its leadership. It wanted to lead Asia to self-sufficiency and prosperity (**www. history.co.uk**).

In 1937, a battle in Beijing, China, became known as the "Marco Polo Bridge Incident." It led to open conflict between Japan and China. Two years later, the war was not going Japan's way, but its imperial ambitions continued. By 1940 (with WWII in full swing in Europe), Japan entered into an alliance with Italy and Germany, putting it further at odds with the United States.

American leaders began to fully support China, and they leveraged economic sanctions against Japan. As the war between China and Japan continued, Japan targeted the oil-rich Dutch East Indies to fuel their actions. In response, the U.S., Britain, and the Netherlands passed an oil embargo on Japan. Their military leaders identified several countries that would be good for resources/oil, but they knew it would mean war with the U.S. (**www.historynet.com**).

The Decision to Bring the U.S. Into the War

The Japanese saw imperial expansion as necessary for their survival. To them, abandoning China was unthinkable, and Southeast Asia was "ripe for rescue, as it was the illegal property of outside colonial powers and within Japan's natural sphere of influence, its manifest destiny," (Weintraub 1991). Still, the decision to go to war with the U.S. or even to attack Pearl Harbor was not unanimous or agreed upon by everyone.

In the fall of 1941, Japan's War Cabinet met. One chief figure was Army leader General Hideki Tojo. He really wanted to take some risk and go to war, but other leaders were more tentative. Most believed that attacking the U.S. was very risky, and not many wanted to attack Pearl Harbor.

Admiral Takijiro Onishi warned that "America could not be 'brought to its knees' by war and that avenues for compromise had to be left open" (Weintraub 1991). The Admiral argued that while landing in the Philippines or somewhere else in the Pacific might work, Hawaii should be avoided. Of course, history tells us he was overruled if not proven incorrect.

As his War Council was arguing over the best thing to do, Emperor Hirohito concluded that while war was a gamble, the Japanese people would not permit them to withdraw from China. He came to believe that diplomatic compromise was doomed to fail and that war seemed inevitable.

Ever since Pearl Harbor was bombed, people have been wondering if President Roosevelt allowed it to happen as a "back door" into the war. In a 1940 election year speech, Roosevelt said, "I have said this before, but I shall say it again and again and again: Your boys are not going to be sent into any foreign wars." However, FDR made it clear to others, including Prime Minister Churchill, that he was determined to help the allies win the war (Perloff 2015).

Of course, a lot of historians say that the idea that Roosevelt allowed the attack on Pearl Harbor to happen is just a silly conspiracy theory. What cannot be denied is that Roosevelt has to share blame in the breakdown of diplomatic relations with Japan.

While supposedly working with Japan to achieve peace, the U.S. did the following things:

- Froze Japanese assets in America

- Closed the Panama Canal to Japanese ships

- Shut down exports to Japan

- Demanded that Japan withdraw all troops from China

You can kind of see why some people think Roosevelt was baiting the Japanese into a fight, right?

Well, whether the U.S. intentionally provoked an attack by Japan to have a reason to enter the war or Japan just arrogantly attacked the U.S. fearing no retaliation, the end result was the same. After that bombing of Pearl Harbor, the entire force of America's industrialization and military was committed to the Allies, and gradually, the tide of the war changed.

A computer-generated 3D illustration of the American battleship USS Arizona.

CHAPTER 3:
THE PLANNING AND EXECUTION OF THE ATTACK

Can you imagine getting your ideas about going to war from a fiction book? It kind of makes you wonder if there is someone out there thinking that *Hunger Games* sounds like an excellent strategy for government. As odd as it sounds, it was Hector Bywater's *The Great Pacific War* (1925) that was Admiral Isoroku Yamamoto's inspiration.

It was a fictional story about a conflict between the U.S. and Japan that began with the Japanese destroying the U.S. fleet. Later in the story, the Japanese attacked Guam and the Philippines. When it was certain that Japan was going to war with the U.S., Yamamoto decided to make Bywater's fiction a reality (**www. nationalww2museum.org**).

The Warnings That Were Ignored

A great deal of planning went into Japan's attack on Pearl Harbor. At the time, Japan and the U.S. were supposed to be trying to reach a diplomatic solution. Even as Japan decided to attack, they made efforts to protect that illusion. They really wanted our leaders to think everything was fine.

Of course, what they didn't know is that American cryptologists had broken the code that they used to send messages to their people in the U.S. in 1940. We had the chance to decode enough information to prevent Pearl Harbor, but somehow, we failed to do so. The messages our people decoded were definitely scary sounding — they warned of a future attack. In that way, we definitely knew something bad was going to happen. Our leaders just didn't think it would happen in Hawaii.

Immediately after the attack, people were looking for someone to blame. The first "scapegoats" (people who take the fall for someone higher up who was really responsible) were Admiral Husband Kimmel, Commander in Chief of the U.S. Pacific Fleet, and Lt. General Walter Short, Commanding General in Hawaii. However, later investigations showed that they were not given proper warnings. So, while Washington was aware of an imminent Japanese attack, the leaders in Hawaii were not (Toland 1982).

What Admiral Kimmel and General Short did know on December 6, 1941 was that war with Japan was not a question of "if," but "when." Because they thought they would soon get called into war, they had prepared their forces for battle. They also knew that a Japanese carrier force had left Japan, disappeared in late November, and was still missing. Still neither commander (nor any of their staff) believed that Pearl Harbor would be Japan's target. Washington D.C. had enough information to warn them that they were in more serious trouble, but before anyone called Hawaii, the attack had begun (Toland 1982).

Perhaps if we hadn't been so overconfident in regards to how safe Pearl Harbor was, maybe the military there would have been more prepared. They might have canceled shore leave (when sailors are allowed the leave the boat and enjoy the place where they are docked — that could mean going to a restaurant, dancing, or a movie) and taken other warnings more seriously. The problem was that since they weren't expecting an attack, they weren't looking for one. For that reason, the most obvious signs like ships and planes were missed.

On December 6, 1941, the U.S. intercepted a Japanese message asking about ships and berthing positions at Pearl Harbor. The cryptologist gave the message to her superior who said he would get it back to her on Monday, December 8th. The morning of the attack, a radar operator on Oahu saw a large group of airplanes on his screen heading toward the island. His superior told him it was probably a group of B-17 bombers heading to the island. These mistakes only feed the conspiracy theory that our government allowed the attack to happen to get us in the war.

 *Fast Fact:* A conspiracy theory suggests that FDR provoked the Japanese attack so that America could enter the war. Modern historians reject this theory.

However, the truth is that these mistakes are just more obvious when you know what happened. Additionally, 75 years ago, the military was not at high alert on a Sunday morning the way they might have been any other day of the week. Neither the ships in the harbor nor the support facilities on land were operating at full force.

Many sailors and soldiers had been given passes to attend religious services off base. If the Japanese had attacked on a Monday, the response to the bombers might have been far more favorable for the United States.

Instead, through a remarkable series of missed warnings, complacency, and negligence, the fleet at Pearl Harbor was caught completely off-guard despite preparing for battle for months. After flying over Oahu, Captain Mitsuo Fuchida sent the coded message "Tora, Tora, Tora" to Japanese command to confirm that they had definitely achieved a surprise attack (**www.nationalgeographic. com**).

The Day of the Attack

The Japanese fleet had to travel 4,000 miles to get within striking distance of Hawaii. That distance alone was one of

---

Dec. 7th, 1941 on the USS Arizona

Donald Stratton had just finished breakfast on the Arizona. He heard a lot of noise coming from the top of the ship. When he went up to check things out, he saw his shipmates pointing out over the water to a bunch of planes.

"I watched one bank and saw the rising sun symbol under the wings and thought 'Boy, that's the Japanese and they're bombing us!'"

Stratton — who was 19 — ran up and joined other sailors on an anti-aircraft gun.

"We were just firing at all those planes. They were coming in so close I could see the pilots when they went by," he said.

When his ship was hit, fire raged all around him. He and five other sailors escaped on a rope to another ship. They had to go hand over hand across 100 feet as all hell was breaking loose around them.

"My hands were burned so badly I don't have any fingerprints," Stratton said.

Stratton spent 10 months in military hospitals getting better. Burns cover 70 percent of his body. Still, he kept serving in the Navy. He was at the battles at New Guinea, Philippines, and Okinawa (Dodd 2014).

the reasons people thought Pearl Harbor was safe. How in the world did they travel so far without anyone noticing? They didn't take a direct path, and they were prepared to destroy any ship that saw them. It just turns out that they got lucky (a luck the U.S. would later mirror), and none of that happened.

The thing is if you want to really mess up a navy, hitting ships at a place where they are all gathered close together with hundreds of airplanes nearby is kind of irresistible. No matter how dangerous or risky the attack at Pearl Harbor was, Japan just had to try. Their task force was made up of six aircraft carriers (with more than 400 airplanes), two battleships, and two heavy cruisers. They also sent a light cruiser, multiple destroyers, and several submarines ahead to clear the way if they ran into any trouble (**www.ww2pacific.com**).

> ### Dec. 7th, 1941 on the USS Maryland
>
> Clarence Pfundheller was standing in front of his ship locker when a shipmate told him the Japanese were attacking them. His friend had been known to stretch the truth, but Pfundheller said, **"Once you seen him, you knew he wasn't lying."**
>
> Not that day.
>
> At 21, Pfundheller ran up to the top of the ship and took control of an anti-aircraft gun. He struggled to see the Japanese planes through tons of smoke. **"You could see them pumping their fists and laughing at you,"** he said (McAvoy 2011).

The air attack on Pearl Harbor was led by Commander Mitsuo Fuchida. The first wave included 183 fighters, bombers, and torpedo bombers. It began slightly before 8 a.m. that Sunday morning.

- At 7:55 a.m., the attack began as dive-bombers stuck the air fields near Pearl Harbor hoping to prevent a U.S. counterattack in the air. Most U.S. planes were parked wingtip-to-wingtip in neat rows to guard against sabotage. They were easily destroyed.

- At 8:10 a.m., an armor-piercing bomb hit the forward deck of the *USS Arizona*. More than 1,000 sailors died in that explosion. The battleship sunk in less than ten minutes.

- At 8:17 a.m., the *Helm*, a U.S. destroyer, left the channel and attacked an enemy submarine. One of the Japanese crewmen died, and the other was captured.

- At 8:39 a.m., the *Monaghan*, a U.S. destroyer, hit an enemy sub with gunfire, rammed it, and sunk it.

- At 8:50 a.m., the *USS Nevada* was hit by bombers hoping to sink it in the channel and trap the fleet. Instead, the crew deliberately grounded the ship.

The second wave of that attack included 170 fighters and bombers; it hit the harbor at 8:54 a.m. By this time, the sailors had a chance to fight back, and those planes were hit by heavy anti-aircraft fire.

- At 8:55 a.m., bombers attacked the navy yard dry dock and hit the *USS Pennsylvania* and two destroyers, the *Cassin* and *Downes*. They also hit the light cruiser *Raleigh*.

- At 9:30 a.m., a bomb blew off the bow of the *Shaw*, a destroyer.

- At 10:00 a.m., Japanese fighters met with bombers off Oahu and flew back to the carriers.

A third wave of attacks was discussed so that Japan could hit gasoline tanks at Pearl Harbor. That didn't happen, because their commanders were very concerned about the missing U.S. carriers. They decided the mission was a success, and at 1 p.m., they set sail for Japanese waters (**www.nationalgeographic. com**).

On December 7, 1941, 51 airplanes were at Hickam Field, and 12 B-17s were expected that day. The first wave of the Japanese attack targeted battleships and carriers as well as the airplanes. For that reason, the first casualties of the bombing were the 35 servicemen having breakfast at the Hickam Field dining hall.

The B-17s did arrive in the middle of the attack, but they couldn't help, because they had no fuel. Hangers and several other base facilities were hit or destroyed. The air field's casualties totaled 121 dead with 274 wounded (**www.nps.gov/nr/travel/ aviation/hic.htm**).

If you've ever seen pictures from the Pearl Harbor attack, you probably saw the damage done to the *USS Arizona*. It was one of the only ships destroyed that day that was not later repaired. In fact, it is still in Pearl Harbor as a war memorial. More than 1,175 people were killed on the *Arizona* alone. One witness from the *USS Nevada* said that the *Arizona* was broken in two before it sunk (**www.historylearningsite.co.uk**).

 *Fast Fact:* 23 sets of brothers died on the *USS Arizona*.

Building burning at Hickam Field

While the U.S. Navy and nearby Hickam Field were surprised by the attack, they were still able to respond. As the fires and destruction raged, the sailors and soldiers did their jobs and fought back. The attack only lasted two hours, but the servicemen brought down 29 Japanese planes and sunk five midget submarines.

Of course, things were far worse for the Americans. U.S. casualties at Pearl Harbor were more than 2,400. Only 129 Japanese soldiers were killed during that attack, and one was taken prisoner. Those numbers make it look like the attack was a great victory for Japan. Maybe it was for a moment. However, they ultimately failed to do the kind of damage they were hoping for, and it was just a matter of time before the U.S. Navy recovered.

Planes being bombed as they sat "wingtip to wingtip"

 *Fast Fact:* The attack on Pearl Harbor lasted about 2 hours.

How the Attack on Pearl Harbor Impacted the U.S. Navy

The ship based at or near Pearl Harbor on the day of the Japanese attack included 8 battleships, 2 heavy cruisers, 6 light cruisers, 29 destroyers, 4 submarines, and several minesweepers and minelayers (**www.history.navy.mil**). While all eight battleships were sunk or badly damaged, several were raised, repaired, and rejoined the fleet during the war. Other classes of ships — such as cruisers and destroyers — were less damaged and rejoined the war rather quickly (**www.pearlharbor.org**).

The damage at Hickam Field

Battleship Row the day of the attack

USS Arizona

USS California

*A Japanese plane and midget submarine destroyed
in the U.S. response effort.*

A Japanese plane shot down during the fighting

Another view of Pearl Harbor under attack

DAMAGED SHIPS AT PEARL HARBOR

SORTED BY NAME, TYPE, AND FATE:

Ship Name	Ship Type	Status on December 7th	Later Action
USS Arizona	Battleship	Sunk	Not Recovered
USS Aylwin	Destroyer	Minor Damage	Repaired by Jan. 1942
USS Bagley	Destroyer	Very Minor Damage	Did not leave action
USS California	Battleship	Sunk	Rebuilt by Jan. 1944
USS Cassin	Destroyer	Damaged in Dry Dock	Rebuilt by Feb. 1944
USS Cummings	Destroyer	Very Minor Damage	Did not leave action
USS Downes	Destroyer	Heavily Damaged	Rebuilt by Nov. 1943
USS Helena	Light Cruiser	Heavily Damaged	Repaired by mid-1942
USS Henley	Destroyer	Very Minor Damage	Did not leave action
USS Honolulu	Light Cruiser	Minor Damage	Repaired by Jan. 1942
USS Hull	Destroyer	Very Minor Damage	Did not leave action
USS Maryland	Battleship	Damaged	Repaired by Feb. 1942
USS Nevada	Battleship	Heavily Damaged	Repaired by Oct. 1942
USS New Orleans	Heavy Cruiser	Minor Damage	Repaired by Feb. 1942
USS Oklahoma	Battleship	Sunk	Not recovered
USS Oglala	Minelayer	Sunk but Salvaged	Re-commissioned Feb. 1944
USS Pennsylvania	Battleship	Damaged in Dry Dock	Repaired by March 1942
USS Raleigh	Light Cruiser	Damaged by Torpedo	Repaired by Feb. 1942
USS Shaw	Destroyer	Heavily Damaged	Repaired by July 1942
USS St. Louis	Light Cruiser	Very Minor Damage	Did not leave action
USS Tennessee	Battleship	Minor Damage	Repaired by Feb. 1942
USS West Virginia	Battleship	Sunk	Rebuilt by July 1944

This list actually looks pretty bad, but remember that less than half of the Navy's total ships were at Pearl Harbor. Of those that were damaged, some only needed minor repairs.

 *Fast Fact:* Six of the eight ships that sunk in Pearl Harbor were fixed and used in WWII.

Another thing that this list doesn't really factor in is how many new ships the Navy had under construction. For example, the *USS Saratoga* had just left dry dock and was entering San Diego when Pearl Harbor was attacked. That aircraft carrier quickly joined the war in the Pacific. The *Saratoga* was important at the battle of Iwo Jima.

Japan also seemed to forget how quickly the Panama Canal allowed the U.S. to transfer ships from their Atlantic Fleet to the Pacific. The *USS Yorktown* was in Norfolk, Virginia in late 1941, but the ship quickly left and arrived in San Diego by January 1, 1942. Among other missions, the *Yorktown* was present at the Battle of Coral Sea and the Battle of Midway.

Even ships as far away as Iceland (the battleships *U.S.S. Mississippi* and *USS Idaho*) were able to leave two days after Pearl Harbor and arrive in San Francisco by January 22, 1942 (**www.ww2pacific.com**).

Even though all the battleships at Pearl Harbor were severely damaged, there were dozens of ships in other classes that were completely unharmed.

Unharmed ships at Pearl Harbor:

Ship Name	Ship Type
USS Allen	Destroyer
USS Blue	Destroyer
USS Bobolink	Minesweeper
USS Cachalot	Submarine
USS Case	Destroyer
USS Chew	Destroyer
USS Conyngham	Destroyer
USS Dale	Destroyer
USS Detroit	Light Cruiser
USS Dewey	Destroyer
USS Dolphin	Submarine
USS Farragut	Destroyer
USS Grebe	Minesweeper
USS Jarvis	Destroyer
USS MacDonough	Destroyer
USS Monaghan	Destroyer
USS Mugford	Destroyer
USS Narwhal	Submarine
USS Patterson	Destroyer
USS Phelps	Destroyer
USS Phoenix	Light Cruiser
USS Rail	Minesweeper
USS Ralph Talbot	Destroyer
USS Reid	Destroyer
USS San Francisco	Heavy Cruiser
USS Schley	Destroyer
USS Selfridge	Destroyer
USS Tautog	Submarine
USS Tern	Minesweeper
USS Tucker	Destroyer
USS Turkey	Minesweeper
USS Vireo	Minesweeper
USS Worden	Destroyer

These destroyers and cruisers proved very important, as they became escorts for the most important type of ship in WWII: aircraft carriers. The most fortunate thing for America was that of the eight carriers that were in commission on December 7, 1941, none of them were at Pearl Harbor.

The *USS Ranger* was returning to Norfolk, Virginia where the *USS Yorktown* and *U.S.S. Long Island* were based. The *USS Hornet* was undergoing training cruises in the Atlantic during that time, and the *USS Wasp* was anchored in Grassy Bay, Bermuda.

In the Pacific, the *USS Saratoga* was just coming out of dry dock. The two carriers that should have been at Pearl Harbor — the *USS Lexington* and *USS Enterprise* — were both at sea with their return being delayed because of storms (McKillop 2016).

The USS Lexington *and* Enterprise *off the coast of Oahu, Hawaii, near Diamond Head.*

With the nature of war changing during WWII, the devastation the U.S. battleships experienced at Pearl Harbor ended up being far less important than the carriers being unharmed.

Air combat was not only important in the attack against Pearl Harbor, but it would be very important in all other Pacific battles. If Japan had sunk any of the Navy's carriers, their success would have been much greater. As events played out, the U.S. Navy was not as damaged as Japan had hoped.

 *Fast Fact:* The crew on the *USS Arizona* was taken by surprise, because they were allowed to sleep late the morning of the attack. Why? They won a dance contest the night before.

The man behind the attack — Admiral Yamamoto — later said, "I fear all we have done is to awaken a sleeping giant and fill him with a terrible resolve."

Admiral Chester W. Nimitz, photographed circa 1942.
(Photo credit: National Archives photo # 80-G-466244)

HOW ADMIRAL NIMITZ SAW PEARL HARBOR

Try staying positive for an entire day. Be affirmative about everything, greet everyone with a smile, attack every task that comes your way with vim and vigor. It's tough. Negativity will be constantly trying to creep its way in.

Now, imagine trying to stay positive in the face of death and tragedy — in the face of an attack like Pearl Harbor. That brings us to the story of Admiral Chester Nimitz.

Nimitz was attending a concert in Washington D.C on Dec. 7, 1941, when he received a phone call from the president of the United States. Franklin Delano Roosevelt himself was on the line.

Japanese forces had attacked Pearl Harbor, the base that Nimitz had overseen the construction of two decades earlier. America was joining World War II, and Roosevelt wanted Nimitz, an expert in submarine warfare and seventh in his class at the Naval Academy, to take command of the Pacific Fleet.

Nimitz organized his staff and prepared to assume command of the fleet. He arrived at Pearl Harbor on Christmas Eve of 1941. He was met with an overwhelming spirit of gloom and despair. It felt like the Japanese had already won the war.

The next day, Nimitz was given a tour of the decimated naval base. Battleships and navy vessels lay damaged and destroyed, cluttering the waters. Things looked really grim.

The story goes like this: Upon returning to the dock after the tour, a young helmsman asked Nimitz what he thought. Nimitz, apparently, responded with confidence and pride.

"The Japanese have made three of the biggest mistakes an attack force could ever make, or God was taking care of America," he said. "Which do you think it was?"

The young helmsman responded quizzically.

"What do you mean by saying the Japanese made the three biggest mistakes an attack force ever made?" he asked.

Nimitz explained: "One. The Japanese attacked on a Sunday morning. Nine out of every ten crewmen of those ships were ashore on leave. If those same ships had been lured to sea and been sunk — we would have lost 38,000 men instead of 3,800.

Two. When the Japanese saw all those battleships lined in a row, they got so carried away sinking those battleships, they never once bombed our dry docks opposite those ships. If they had destroyed our dry docks, we would have had to tow every one of those ships to America to be repaired. As it is now, the ships are in shallow water and can be raised. One tug can pull them over to the dry docks, and we can have them repaired and at sea by the time we could have towed them to America. And I already have crews ashore anxious to man those ships.

Three. Every drop of fuel in the Pacific theater of war is in top of the ground storage tanks five miles away over that hill. One attack plane could have strafed those tanks and destroyed our fuel supply.

That's why I say the Japanese made three of the biggest mistakes an attack force could make, or God was taking care of America."

His positive outlook was proven right. America defeated Japan in the Pacific Theater and continued its path to the country it is today.

Nimitz, along with Army General Douglas MacArthur, is credited by historians as one of the two most important men in the outcome of the Pacific. At the signing of the Japanese Instrument of Surrender, they were the first two men to sign the document for the U.S.

I wonder if the paper had silver lining.

CHAPTER 4:
GOING TO WAR

After the attack at Pearl Harbor, Congress immediately declared war on Japan. Since Germany had an alliance with Japan, it declared war on the U.S. along with Italy and other members of the Axis powers. With a bombing that lasted less than a couple of hours, American resistance to entering World War II came to end.

What happens in a U.S. territory right after a huge bombing that got the country into a war? Well, martial law of course! If you're unfamiliar with the term, martial law is basically the government taking over every aspect of your life. Picture being "grounded" by the U.S. Army instead of your mom or dad.

General Short pushed Hawaii's Governor Joseph Poindexter to declare martial law, and President Roosevelt supported the idea. Believing it would end quickly, the governor agreed. However, despite the fact that there were no additional attacks, martial law continued in Hawaii until the end of the war.

As a result of martial law, a military governor replaced Poindexter, and military tribunals replaced the court system. In a lot of ways, the U.S. military controlled daily life in Hawaii. During this time, wages were frozen, bars and restaurants were regulated, curfews were set, the press was censored, and rent prices were controlled (**http://hawaii-guide.info**).

Can you imagine living in such a situation? The military told you what you were allowed to do and when you were allowed to do it. Everyone had to be home by a certain time of day (parents, kids, everyone!). If there had been social media, it would have been cut off. The Army was in charge — end of story. Life was hard for all Hawaiians after the bombing, but it was worse for the Japanese-Americans living there. Paradise had temporarily changed entirely.

The U.S. Response to Pearl Harbor

One of the reasons why the attack at Pearl Harbor seemed to be a huge victory for Japan is becuase of several military successes it had after.

First, Guam and Wake Island fell to the Japanese. Then, the Dutch East Indies, Hong Kong, Malaya, Singapore, and Burma all lost to them as well. At the time, it seemed like Japan was on a roll, and the American people didn't feel very good about the war ahead.

 *Fast Fact:* During the attack, Navy cook Doris "Dorie" Miller, went beyond his call of duty. Even though he was never trained for combat, he fired a machine gun until he ran out of ammunition, shooting down three to four Japanese planes. He became the first African-American to be awarded the Navy Cross.

President Roosevelt felt that the best victory would be counterstrike for Pearl Harbor. On December 21, 1941, he held a meeting with his military commanders at the White House demanding a bombing raid on Japan as soon as possible. The U.S. didn't want to risk losing another ship, but it knew the President was right, so it went to work on a plan to bomb Japan.

Admiral Ernest J. King, Commander in Chief of the U.S. Navy, agreed with Roosevelt's idea, but he wasn't sure how to make it happen. A member of his staff suggested they fly Army bombers off a carrier. This had never been done before. Aircraft carriers weren't really designed to launch plans that big. However, it was such a good idea that they wanted to see if it was possible.

The Navy tested the plan on a runway in Virginia painted with the dimensions of a carrier deck. They figured out that the B-25B Mitchell medium bomber was the best plane for the mission, and went for it. This plane was new to combat, so the Navy trained a whole crew on how to fly them — particularly how to fly them off of an aircraft carrier. It also trained the crew without telling them what the mission was. Talk about difficult!

Not only was the plane new, but the mission was carried out on the *Hornet,* a newly built ship. Everything about the mission symbolized why the U.S. bounced back after Pearl Harbor — **new ships, new planes, and new tactics.** It was even a young (probably teenage crew) that traveled from Virginia through the Panama Canal to San Francisco and eventually on to Japan.

One of the only things about this mission that wasn't new was its commander, the veteran pilot Lt. Col. James H. Doolittle. He was an ace pilot who had broken the world record of flying 296 miles an hour in 1932. When he was given command of this operation, he recruited 140 flyers from the 17th Bombardment Group. He gathered his group of pilots at Eglin Field in the Florida Panhandle. On the first day, he asked for volunteers for an "extremely hazardous" mission that would be "the most dangerous thing any of you have ever done." Every recruit stayed with the mission knowing no more than that (Horne 2012).

The pilots went through a month of intense, top secret training where they learned to take off in a B-25 in as little as 287 feet. To accomplish this difficult task, they had to re-learn a lot of what they knew about flying. It wasn't easy, and it was very risky. Two planes crashed during training. The remaining planes were modified to reduce their weight.

Because the chance of the pilots successfully landing their planes after their bombing run was very low, the military removed a lot of special equipment. For example, top-secret and highly accurate Norden bombsights were removed from the planes to prevent the technology from falling into Japanese hands. Also, three extra fuel tanks were added, and the pilots were given five-gallon jerry cans of fuel to top their tanks off by hand. This was very unusual and it probably worried the pilots more than any other part of their training.

The need for so much fuel signaled the most dangerous part of their mission. The pilots were not just going to take off from the *Hornet* and bomb the island of Japan. They were also going to fly over Japan and land in nearby Russia or China. Since Russians were unwilling to go to war with Japan at the time, the Soviet government refused to let the pilots land in Siberia. That meant the pilots had to make it all the way to China, and they would need every drop of fuel to do it.

After all their training, the bombing force was made up of 15 B-25s (with five crew members each). Doolittle got that number up to 16, because he insisted on leading the mission in the air. He also wanted to be the first plane off the carrier, which meant he had the least amount of space for takeoff. Basically, he refused to let any of his men take more risk than he did.

The B-25s on the USS Hornet on the way to Japanese waters

In April of 1942, Doolittle, his men, and the B-25s sailed out of San Francisco Bay on the *Hornet* into the Pacific Ocean. That's when the Navy crew and Army pilots finally learned what their mission was.

The *Hornet* was joined by the *USS Enterprise*, four cruisers, eight destroyers, and two fleet oilers. At one point, they were spotted by a Japanese picket boat, and they promptly sunk it. However, it did send the message that an enemy naval force was close to Japanese waters. For some reason, the Japanese didn't react. Still, Doolittle and the ship captain believed the mission was in danger. For that reason, they launched early, 170 miles further away than planned.

All 16 planes successfully launched, and the task force headed back to Hawaii. It was a very dangerous six hour flight to Japan. Doolittle later reported that at one point, he saw nine Japanese Zeros flying above them in a V formation, but nothing happened. The B-25s must have been mistaken for Japanese bombers.

The team flew at what is described as "wave-top" level (basically really close to the ocean) to avoid detection. They reached the coast of Japan at noon their time. In single file and at low altitudes, Doolittle's men dropped bombs on military targets in Tokyo, Yokohama, Kobe, and Osaka. The raid was over in a matter of minutes with no one being shot down. The damage to Japan was also minimal, but the important thing was that they had hit back at Japan. When the news broke, people celebrated.

It was a long time before that story broke. They didn't have Internet or 24/7 news stations back then. Also, the pilots had a long and very dangerous journey before they would get back home.

Photo # NH 97502   LtCol. Doolittle and crewmen in China after April 1942 raid on Japan

Doolittle and members of his crew with Chinese officials after the 1942 air raid. Pictured left to right: Staff Sgt. Fred A. Braemer, bombardier; Staff Sgt. Paul Leonard, flight engineer and gunner; General Ho, Director of Branch Government of Western Chekiang Province; Lt. Richard E. Cole, copilot; Doolittle; Henry H. Shen, bank manager; Lt. Henry A. Potter, navigator; Chao Foo Ki, secretary of Western Chekiang Province Branch Government.

After they dropped their bombs, the pilots flew west to China. All of the pilots had flown a record 2,250 miles in 13 hours. Night was approaching, and they were all extremely low on fuel. Doolittle knew that he could not reach the Chinese airfield they were aiming for, so he ordered his crew to bail out. They got lucky and parachuted down into a rice paddy. The following day, they found a Chinese military patrol, and they were soon on their way home.

Every one of the 16 planes was lost, but most of the pilots and crews were able to bail out in Chinese-controlled areas. Not all were so lucky, though. One bomber crash-landed in Soviet territory, and two came down in Japanese-controlled areas. Some of the pilots and crew died, were imprisoned, or were executed. All 80 men received the Distinguished Flying Cross. Doolittle was also awarded the Congressional Medal of Honor (Horne 2012).

In terms of finances and lives, the cost of the mission for the U.S. was high, but it was still a great moral victory. Prior to Pearl Harbor, most people did not want to join WWII. While the attack changed people's minds, all the bad news coming from the Pacific was depressing the American people as well as the soldiers fighting the war. That's why Doolittle's raid was so important. It gave people hope that we could win, and strengthened our fighting spirit.

U.S. Involvement in Europe and Africa

Because war with Japan also meant war with Germany and Italy, the U.S. quickly deployed troops and supplies to Europe and Africa. Enrollment in the armed forces skyrocketed during WWII as did manufacturing of airplanes and warships. Also, thousands of women served in the Army and Navy or worked in factories to support the war. Simply put, the entire country got into the war movement.

The U.S. contribution in Africa was limited, but effective. The turning point in the Desert War came at the Battle of Tunisia. Allied forces comprised mostly of U.S. and UK soldiers defeated the Germans and Italians and took more than 275 thousand prisoners of war into custody. Hitler was too busy with Russia to properly support Italy, and the Allies soon won. By September of 1943, Italy had officially surrendered.

The U.S. contributions to the War in Europe were much more involved. One of the biggest victories was at the Battle of Normandy in June of 1944 when U.S., British, and Canadian forces fought back German troops occupying France. Six months later, at the Battle of the Bulge, the U.S. Army fought the largest battle in its history, with the worst casualties in a single battle. More than 80,000 American soldiers were wounded or died at the Battle of the Bulge, but it served as the last major German offensive on the Western Front (**www.u-s-history.com**).

 *Fast Fact:* According to History.com, German troops pretended to be members of the U.S. Army by wearing stolen U.S. Army uniforms.

After the Allies defeated the German army in the Ardennes, there was a push by both the Americans and the Soviets to reach Berlin. The result was that Germany fell by May of 1945. The war in Europe and Africa was much more detailed than this section covers, but since the most direct impact of Pearl Harbor was the war in the Pacific, this book will concentrate on those aspects of World War II.

The War in the Pacific

In the early days of the war in the Pacific, Japan quickly conquered Guam, Wake Island, Dutch East Indies, Hong Kong, Malaysia, Singapore, and Burma. Japan secured new territories even as the U.S. celebrated Doolittle's bombing. That started to change by mid-1942. Many historians consider the subsequent Battle of Midway, which took place in June of 1942, to be the turning point of the war against Japan (**www.ushmm.org**).

Prior to the Battle of Midway, Admiral Yamamoto invaded a target relatively close to Pearl Harbor to draw out the American fleet. No one is really sure why he did it. Maybe it was in response to Doolittle's raid, or maybe he just wanted to sink the aircraft carriers he missed at Pearl Harbor. Either way, he thought that when the U.S. began a counterattack, the Japanese would crush what remained of their Pacific fleet.

What Yamamoto did not know was that U.S. intelligence broke the Japanese fleet codes and knew his exact plan. Instead of drawing out the U.S. fleet, he was taken by surprise. Commander Admiral Chester W. Nimitz placed U.S. carriers in position to attack the Japanese as they prepared to attack Midway Island. During the battle that followed, the Americans sank four Japanese carriers that helped carry out the attack on Pearl Harbor. The Japanese also lost more than 300 aircraft and a heavy cruiser (**www.history.com**).

Other historians believe the turning point of the war came with the U.S. victory at Guadalcanal in February of 1943. In August of 1942, the U.S. Marines launched a surprise attack in the Solomon Islands (of which Guadalcanal is part of). They fought hard to take control of an air base under construction, but it wasn't an easy victory.

Over the next few months, several land and sea battles took place. The Japanese lost two-thirds of the 31,400 troops committed to the island. Ship losses on both sides were heavy, but the most significant damage was done to Japan's aircraft (**www.history. com**).

Late in 1944, Americans liberated the Philippines and began massive air strikes on Japan. In the early months of 1945, the U.S. suffered heavy losses as they invaded Iwo Jima in February and Okinawa in April. During this time, the Japanese started suicidal air attacks known as Kamikaze attacks. This may have been a sign that Japan was losing, but it also showed how hard it would be to get the Japanese to surrender.

The End of the War with Japan

On August 6, 1945, President Harry Truman informed the world that an atomic bomb had been dropped on the Japanese city Hiroshima. Three days later, a second bomb was dropped on Nagasaki. The two attacks killed nearly 200,000 people. Neither city was a strategic military target, so the casualties were largely civilians.

 *Fast Fact:* The plane that carried the bomb to Hiroshima was named "Enola Gay," after the pilot's mother. There were cyanide pills (suicide pills) for the crew to take if the mission failed.

Since use of the atomic bomb was completely new, there were long-term effects that no one could predict. The bombings achieved their desired purpose. Six days after Nagasaki was hit, the Japanese surrendered, and WWII was over.

The Atomic bomb was not originally developed with Japan in mind. Early in 1939, German physicists discovered how to split a uranium atom. Fear spread that the Nazis would soon be able to create a more powerful bomb than anyone could imagine. Albert Einstein, who escaped the Nazis, and Enrico Fermi, who escaped fascist Italy, were then living in the U.S. They convinced President Roosevelt to support an atomic research program called the Manhattan Project.

The Manhattan Project might have been the biggest top secret program in U.S. history. It employed more than 120,000 people and cost nearly $2 billion dollars. However, the people who knew exactly what the project was for were limited to a select few. The Americans didn't even tell Allied leader Joseph Stalin what they were working on. Even more surprising, Vice President Truman was completely left out of the loop. It wasn't until he was sworn in as President that they told him about the project (**www.ushistory.org**).

The Manhattan Project was successful in its secrecy and its purpose. However, by the summer of 1945 when the bomb was ready, Germany had already surrendered (May 7, 1945). As a result, even though the Manhattan Project had begun to fight the Nazis, the only target the bomb would be needed for was Japan.

Truman's decision to use the bomb on Japan has been questioned and criticized ever since. There are analysts that insist Japan was going to fall, and the bombings were unnecessary. Truman and the U.S. were accused of racism. People said they would have never bombed Germany liked that. It's impossible to know what would have happened if the bomb had been ready earlier. There was a lot of ill-will toward Japan still because of Pearl Harbor. Yet, Truman always said his decision to bomb Japan was just a strategic one.

 *Fast Fact:* The bomb dropped on Hiroshima was named "Little Boy."

Truman argued that his decision to drop the bomb probably saved Japanese and American lives. The fire bombing raids that were going on at the time killed more Japanese civilians than the initial deaths from the Atomic bombs. From that point of view, Truman was right. The problem is that neither Truman nor the scientists of the day understood the radiation sickness that would follow (**www.ushistory.org**).

Fast Fact: The bomb dropped on Nagasaki was named "Fat Man."

Those who defend Truman's choice say that using the bomb ended the war at the earliest possible moment. Some say he did it to justify the huge cost of the Manhattan Project. Others say he did it to intimidate the Soviets.

Certain considerations, however, relate directly to December 7th, 1941. When people objected to using the Atomic bomb, other decision makers brought up Pearl Harbor. They said Japan broke the "rules of war" there, so this was a fair thing to do. From the Japanese perspective, honor was considered sacrosanct (very, very important!). However, many Americans thought they were cheaters and deserved extra punishment (Donohue 2012).

In the end, the biggest reason Truman may have used the bomb was that there was just no objection to it. If the U.S. had been brought into war against the Japanese in any other way than the attack on Pearl Harbor, maybe people would have objected more. As is, we can conclude that Pearl Harbor made those who ordered the attacks on Hiroshima and Nagasaki feel justified.

HEROES OF PEARL HARBOR

For the many survivors of the attacks on Pearl Harbor, there were over twice as many deaths that occurred on that horrific day. Though tragedy ensued in the wake of the bombings, all military branches were able to spotlight heroes that showed tremendous courage when it came to protecting their comrades and civilians. Here are a few heroes that died at the hands of the Japanese during that surprise attack on December, 7th 1941:

Hickok, Warren Paul—

As a member of the US Navy, Hickok was assigned aboard *USS Sicard*, one of the many light mine layers in Pearl Harbor. Shortly thereafter, Hickok was dispatched along with most of the men from the *Sicard* to help the crew members of the *USS Cummings*, a destroyer that was docked not too far away. Either by miscommunication or purposed intent, Hickok boarded the *USS Pennsylvania* as the attacks began. The *USS Cummings* was able to get clear of Pearl Harbor without reporting a single injury. As for the *USS Pennsylvania*, this battleship was noted to have fired at the enemy first. Though this battleship did not take on as much damage as the other ships, 15 men were killed, 14 went missing in action, and 38 were wounded. Of these men, Hickok was one of the 14 missing in action. Initially, his death was not listed on the *Pennsylvania* draft. During the aftermath of the attacks, an overwhelming majority of bodies were not recognizable to the public and were buried in Nuuanu Cemetery. But in 2005, with the help of Pearl Harbor survivor Ray Emory, local officials were able to find Hickok's remains for a proper burial.

Navy Seaman 2nd Class Warren Paul Hickok;
Photo courtesy of the U.S. Department of Defense.

Jones, Herbert C.—

Herbert Jones began his career as a young officer in the Navy. Jones brought his wife with him to be stationed in Honolulu. Joanne was in the officer's quarters when the attack on Pearl Harbor began. Jones was to relieve the officer-in-charge aboard the *USS California* when the bombers flew overheard. The Japanese had planned to fire torpedoes shortly after the aircraft bombings. It was later reported that Jones kept going down into the battleship after the ship was hit by a torpedo to rescue the crew members. On his fourth or fifth trip down to the hull of the *USS California*, another torpedo made contact with the ship, and Jones was killed instantly. Herbert Jones was given the Medal of Honor for his selfless dedication to the lives of others. An *Edsell* class destroyer was later named after him.

Navy Lieutenant Herbert C. Jones
U.S. Naval History and Heritage Command Photograph.

Sterling, Gordon H. Jr.—

Gordon was stationed in Pearl Harbor as a member of the Air Force. Of the many Air Force soldiers, he was one of the few pilots that were able to take off. He was able to gun down at least one Japanese aircraft before being shot down by another. He perished in the water after his aircraft sunk. Unfortunately for his family and friends, his body was not recoverable. His funeral ceremony was given at the Arlington Cemetery for this brave second lieutenant.

CHAPTER 5:
THE RESULTS OF PEARL HARBOR FOR JAPAN

Even though Admiral Yamamoto planned the attack on Pearl Harbor, he told the Emperor ahead of time that he couldn't predict the outcome of a full-scale war with the United States. Yamamoto said that he thought he could fight the U.S. successfully for six months to one year. After that, nothing was guaranteed. If war was inevitable, Yamamoto said it would be best to go big and "cripple the Americans." He thought if that attack worked, the U.S. would be willing to negotiate peace.

Months before the attack at Pearl Harbor, Yamamoto made this prediction: "For a while we'll have everything our own way, stretching out in every direction like an octopus spreading its tentacles. But it'll last for a year and a half at the most," (**https://pearlharboroahu.com**).

It turns out Yamamoto's prediction was correct. From that point of view, he was successful at Pearl Harbor. Unfortunately, the end result was not what he wanted. For that reason, you might ask if the attack was worth it. Japan would probably say no. However, 75 years later, Japan has recovered much of their strength — they are an economic superpower, and their military ranks pretty high as well.

Was Pearl Harbor a Success for Japan?

Japan had three goals when they attacked Pearl Harbor: cripple the Pacific Fleet, increase their hold on Asian territories, and negotiate an armistice from a position of strength. Unfortunately, they were wrong about the U.S.'s willingness to negotiate after such an attack. They also may not have understood how much President Roosevelt wanted to get involved in WWII anyway.

So, did they fail? Well, they did conquer a lot of Asian territories after Pearl Harbor. However, they were completely unable to negotiate anything with the United States. Most importantly, as discussed in previous chapters, they didn't damage the U.S. fleet as much as they had hoped (**www.historynet.com**).

Beyond the failure to sink the Navy's aircraft carriers, the long-term damage to the fleet was minimal. Even though all the battleships suffered damage during the attack, three were back in action within one month. On the other hand, by the end of WWII, all of the Japanese aircraft carriers and capital ships used to attack Pearl Harbor had been sunk. (**www.historylearningsite. co.uk**).

The truth is that Pearl Harbor could have been worse for America. If fuel storage tanks had been destroyed, operations in the Pacific would have been slowed. Also, ship repair and servicing installations at Pearl Harbor were quickly brought back up to speed. Finally, the U.S.'s ability to control and make use of the Panama Canal allowed the Navy to quickly rebound.

The most alarming question for Japan is whether or not America would have gone to war with them at all if they did not initiate an attack. While war seemed necessary for the Japanese, most

Photo # NH 83056   USS Nevada enters drydock at Pearl Harbor, 18 Feb. 1942

The USS Nevada *was just one of the battleships that was damaged at Pearl Harbor, but was repaired, modernized, and returned to combat by May of 1943.*

Americans didn't think that way. In fact, most Americans didn't really care about Japan's conquests in the Pacific. A lot of people just wanted to defend our borders and stay out of global conflict. Japan's biggest failure might be that they changed American's minds and made them want to go to war.

What a Difference a Canal Makes!

If you are unfamiliar with the Panama Canal, you might not understand why it was so important to the U.S. winning the war. Since the U.S. turned the canal over to the Panamanian government in 1999 (before most of you were born), you might not realize that the U.S. used to completely control it.

Today, the waterway that connects the Atlantic and Pacific Oceans is extremely important to global trade. In WWII, it helped the U.S. quickly move ships to the Pacific to replace the ones that were lost or damaged at Pearl Harbor. To understand why it was such a big deal, think about how ships used to have to move from the Atlantic to the Pacific. Before the canal opened in 1914, ships had to travel around the southern tip of South America. Now the trip is 11,000 kilometers shorter and is much safer.

 *Fast Fact:* America originally wanted to build the canal in Nicaragua, not Panama.

The U.S. government ended up controlling the Panama Canal for 85 years through a series of coincidences that worked in America's favor. In the 1880s, Ferdinand de Lesseps, the same French engineer who built the Suez Canal in Egypt, tried and failed to build a canal in this area. Several years later, the U.S. supported Panama's efforts to become an independent nation. The new government signed a treaty that gave America the right to build and control a canal in their new borders.

It took a decade to build the canal, and it officially opened in 1914. Many decades later, the U.S. and Panama reached a new agreement that gave the Canal Zone to Panama's government in 1999. However, the U.S. still holds the rights to defend the canal during times of war. Today, 12,000+ ships and 200 million tons of goods pass through the canal every year. During WWII, it saved the U.S. Navy (**www.unmuseum.org**).

 *Fast Fact:* About 25,000 people died while building the canal.

Even prior to war, the U.S. government used the Panama Canal a lot. The first U.S. Navy ship to go through the canal was the *USS Jupiter.* It took nearly two days for the ship to get all the way through. After that, the U.S. used it to spread supplies to all their forces during WWI. In the years that followed, the canal was used for commerce and military purposes (**www. navalhistory.org**).

Even though they didn't want to go to war, the U.S. Congress started growing the Navy again in the 1930s. Under President Roosevelt's leadership, Congress allowed the Navy to increase in strength by 20 percent. At the end of 1933, the Navy had 372 ships. Over the next several years, they added hundreds of ships to their arsenal.

First, the U.S. Congress allowed the Navy to add 65 destroyers, 30 submarines, 1 air craft carrier and more than 1,000 airplanes by 1942. Then, they approved large-scale construction of aircraft carriers, cruisers, and submarines. Finally, Roosevelt got them to let the Navy build 7 battleships, 18 carriers, 115 destroyers, and 42 submarines (**www.globalsecurity.org**).

By the time Pearl Harbor was attacked in 1941, the U.S. was committed to a two-ocean navy. For that reason, the Panama

Canal eventually became less important, but not before it played a vital role in rebuilding the Pacific fleet. A lot of the ships Roosevelt approved were still being built when Pearl Harbor was attacked. As those ships came out of dry dock, the Panama Canal let the Navy quickly get the ships where they wanted them (**www.navalhistory.org**).

A Change in Public Opinion & Prejudices

Roosevelt wanted to enter the war and help the allies, but he had a hard time getting Congress to declare war. As a result, there are those who believe the U.S. government, primarily Roosevelt, allowed the attack on Pearl Harbor to happen to give them a reason to enter the war.

Many people think the idea that a U.S. President would permit an attack on U.S. soil is crazy. Yet, no one can deny that Americans' attitude toward the war changed dramatically after Pearl Harbor. Congress passed resolutions to go to war against all of Axis powers in a matter of days. The U.S. military quickly positioned troops in both Europe and the Pacific.

THE JAPANESE – HAWAIIANS OF WWII

When Japan attacked Pearl Harbor in 1941, more than 160 thousand people of Japanese descent were living in Hawaii. Unlike their counterparts on the mainland, there was no practical way to move them all into internment camps, but with martial law ruling this state, it was a very difficult period for these Japanese-Hawaiians.

After the bombings, many Nisei (Japanese born in Hawaii) wanted to volunteer to serve in the U.S. military. This was not allowed until 1943, but when it was, thousands of Nisei eagerly joined and became the 442nd Infantry. They distinguished themselves in Europe, winning numerous medals and honors. When those who survived returned to Hawaii after the war, they were hailed as heroes.

American's attitudes about the war weren't the only thing that changed. Prejudices changed as well — and not for the better. Some people think racism is just a black and white thing. In reality, racism and prejudices are far more widespread and complex than that. No matter how old you were during the 9/11 attacks, you have probably seen the racism and prejudice that followed.

American culture of the 21st century told us it was wrong to blame all people of Middle Eastern descent for the 9/11 attacks. However, America went through a lot of "growing pains," racial tensions, and mistakes before we got to a culture like that. Even still, it was difficult for some people not to lump all Muslim people into one category.

When the Japanese attacked Pearl Harbor, the negative response was much more extreme (and hateful) than you could probably imagine. Anti-Japanese paranoia became so widespread that people thought all the Japanese in the U.S. were spies. You can imagine how this made the large population of Japanese feel.

People thought that if the Japanese planes had reached the mainland, the Japanese-Americans living on the West Coast would be a security risk. Even though the country was also at war with Germany and Italy, it was the Japanese that people feared the most. To make people feel better, Roosevelt signed an executive order that relocated all Americans of Japanese ancestry to internment camps. More than 127,000 U.S. citizens of Japanese descent were imprisoned in those camps.

Orders were posted in Japanese-American communities that told them where to go and what to do. Families sold their homes, stores, and assets (at considerably less value than they were worth) since they didn't know what the future held. Nearly two-thirds of the people who had to live in those camps were born in the United States. That means they were U.S. born citizens! Most of them had never even been to Japan. Even Japanese-Americans who had been veterans of WWI were forced to relocate.

Ten camps were built in remote areas of seven states. People ate in mess halls (military cafeterias), children attended schools, and adults could work for $5 a day. Most of the camps were built in places that made farming difficult. Life in general was very hard and probably very confusing for younger children.

Fast Fact: In June of 1942, Japan seized two small islands in Alaska: Attu and Kiska. It was the only U.S. soil Japan would claim during the war.

When the camp prisoners were finally released, many did not return to their hometowns. Hostility against Japanese-Americans remained high, especially along the West Coast. In 1988, the U.S. Congress passed legislation to make restitution with camp survivors, paying each interned individual $20,000 (**www.ushistory.org**). It really didn't make up for anything, but at least it was formal recognition that these people were treated unjustly.

Of course, Asian people had experienced discrimination and mistreatment in the U.S. ever since the Chinese first came to America. However, both the Chinese and Japanese had worked hard to make a place for themselves in the U.S., and both had a thriving culture prior to 1941. That all changed with the attack on Pearl Harbor, which "set off an overwhelming wave of racism, prejudice, and ignorance" (**www.asian-nation.org**).

Since America was allied with China in WWII, Chinese-Americans were treated a little better. In 1943, the U.S. allowed Chinese residents to become naturalized citizens. That was great while it lasted, but when China became a communist country, American attitudes changed again. On the other hand, as America worked to rebuild Japan after the war, relations with Japan became more positive. By 1952, Japanese-Americans could also become naturalized citizens, and soon they could be viewed as allies instead of enemies (**www.asian-nation.org**).

In a lot of cases, it really didn't matter if someone was Chinese, Japanese, or from somewhere else in Asia. Many Americans couldn't tell the difference. If they disliked the Chinese, Japanese, Koreans, or Vietnamese; they probably disliked all Asians. The prejudices that were formed during WWII passed on to new generations and got even worse thanks to conflicts in Korea and Vietnam. Today, these negative feelings toward Asians do not seem to be present. In fact, many parts of Asian culture, particularly food, have become very popular in the U.S.

Over time, people of Asian ancestry went from being viewed in a negative light to being viewed as highly intelligent and hard working. The Pew Research Center reports that by 2010, Asian immigrants had risen to 36 percent, passing even the number of Hispanics entering the U.S. each year. While Asian Americans only represent 5.8 percent of the U.S. population, they still now total more than 18 million in all, with excess of 1.3 million individuals being of Japanese descent (**www.pewsocialtrends. org**).

Even Asian-Americans themselves don't feel that discrimination is a significant problem for them. Pew Research Center reports that only 13 percent of Asian-Americans say that they feel discrimination against their group is a major problem, while 48 percent feel it is a minor problem and 35 percent say it is not a problem at all. According to their research, only 20 percent of Asian-Americans say they have been treated unfairly in the past year because of their race, and merely 10 percent report being called an offensive name (**www.pewsocialtrends.org**).

While the immediate response to the attack on Pearl Harbor (the internment camps) was clearly a horrible violation of personal freedom, American feelings about the Japanese have changed a lot in a positive direction over the last 75 years. It's not the best it could be, but like anything, it's getting better.

Post World War II Japan

By the end of WWII, large portions of Europe and Asia were in ruins, and the "spoils" of war still had to be awarded. Borders were redrawn, and a massive effort to rebuild in many war-torn nations was quickly underway. Allied forces took control of Germany, Japan, and much of the territory those nations had conquered during the war.

In Japan, the U.S. led the Allies in helping to rebuild the Japanese state. From 1945 to 1952, General Douglas MacArthur drove military, political, economic, and social reforms. Unlike in

Germany, the Soviets, China, and the UK pretty much let the Americans handle the rebuilding of Japan. Under MacArthur, the occupation of Japan went from an effort to punish and reform to a push to revive their economy and formalize a peace treaty.

Between 1945 and 1947, efforts were made to fundamentally change the Japanese government and society. War crime trials were conducted in Tokyo, the Japanese army was dismantled, and former military officers were banned from becoming political leaders. Also, land reform laws that benefited small-time farmers were passed (**https://history.state.gov**).

In 1947, Allied advisors gave Japan's leaders a new constitution to support. It downgraded the emperor's status to a figurehead and set up a parliamentary system of government. Emperor Hirohito was forced to renounce his divinity and publically supported Japan's new constitu-

---

POST WORLD WAR II GERMANY

In the 75 years since Pearl Harbor was bombed, Berlin fell, was divided, and later reunified. If you are in high school or younger, you were born in a world where the Berlin Wall was nothing but a history lesson. For older Americans, it represented everything about the Cold War.

Berlin was divided into four zones, each controlled by a former allied power: the Soviets, the French, the British, and the Americans. The areas controlled by France, the UK, and the U.S. were united into West Germany. The wall that separated the country was built in the 1960s.

Life was very different on opposite sides of that wall. Greater efforts were made to rebuild West Germany; their citizens had greater freedom. During the Cold War, the country stood as a constant reminder of the conflict between the Soviet Union and the U.S. It would be another 30 years before the country was made whole again. More than 50 years after Germany invaded Poland and started WWII, the wall came down and Germany finally knew peace (**www.history.com**).

tion. For a culture as old as Japan's, this was a huge change. Their new constitution encouraged better rights and privileges for women, it ended their right to wage war, and it disbanded all non-defensive armed forces.

After the political structure of Japan was remade, there was a strong effort to rebuild their economy. This effort was helped by the conflict in Korea, because Japan served as the principal supply depot for UN forces. Beginning in 1950, leaders started working on a formal peace treaty.

Unlike Germany, where the Cold War left the nation divided for many decades, Japan fared much better. This is partially because the U.S. changed their minds about who represented a real threat in the Pacific.

By the 1950s, Americans had come to fear the spread of communism to an almost hysterical level. Paranoia crept into society as McCarthyism led to thousands of Americans being asked the question, "Are you now, or have you ever been, a member of the communist party?"

Senator Joseph McCarthy led investigations to identify communist sympathizers in the U.S. People came to fear not only the presence of communist spies in the country, but also the spread of communism worldwide. Some of this fear made sense. Soviet spies stole the secrets to the Atomic bomb, and Russia tested a bomb in 1949. Our former ally, China, became communistic, and Joseph Stalin expanded the Soviet Union's reach to cover half of Europe (**www.ushistory.org**). Instead of a bitter enemy, the U.S. came to see Japan as an ally in a part of the world where capitalism and democracy were losing.

For that reason, the treaty between the U.S. and Japan was quickly formed. It allowed America to maintain military bases in Okinawa and other parts of Japan. Since Japan was restricted to a Self-Defense Force only (which was formed in 1954), the U.S. promised to defend Japan if they were attacked.

Japan's economy recovered, but was impacted by global trends. They were negatively impacted by the 1973 oil crisis, but responded by shifting from industrialization to a focus on technology. Today, Japan ranks third in terms of Gross Domestic Product (GDP) behind the U.S. and China (**http://databank. worldbank.org**).

In terms of military strength, Japan is listed at number seven on the Global Firepower list for 2015. The ranking order out of 126 countries is the U.S., Russia, China, India, France, the UK, and then Japan. Turkey, Germany, and Italy round out the top ten of that list (**www.globalfirepower.com**). In short, Japan might not have achieved the dominance in the Pacific that they wanted prior to WWII, but they are still a major economic and militaristic power on the world stage.

Japan and the U.S. 75 Years Later

Since the signing of the formal treaty between the U.S. and Japan, relations and investments in each other have only increased. Today, the U.S. State Department refers to the American-Japanese relationship as the "cornerstone of U.S. security interests in Asia" and says they are fundamental to regional stability and prosperity (Jones 2014).

There are still a lot of U.S. military bases in Japan. They include three U.S. Air Force bases, three Army bases, and three Navy fleet bases as well as a naval air facility in Kanagawa, Japan. There are a grand total of 13 Marine Corps camps across the small island of Japan, including one airfield in Okinawa (**www. militarybases.com**). In total, more than 50,000 U.S. military personnel serve in Japan every year.

As of August of 2015, Japan held more U.S. government debt than any other country. This essentially means that Japan owns a large part of our national debt and is tied very closely to us in terms of economic well-being.

As Japan shifted from being a heavily oil-dependent country in the 1970s to more technologically focused, their corporations grew into global powerhouses.

Chances are, you have a Japanese product, or several, in your home. From the cars (Toyota or Honda) to the game systems or computers (Sony or Nintendo) to the televisions (Panasonic), Japanese products are part of everyday life in America. While Americans have done their part to make Japanese companies successful across the globe, the Japanese also spend millions of dollars on American products each year. In 2015, the U.S. exported

Top Ten Global Japanese Companies
1. Toyota (Automobile)
2. Mitsubishi Financial (Banking)
3. Sumitomo Mitsui Financial (Banking)
4. Nippon Telegraph & Tel (Telecom)
5. Honda (Automobile)
6. Softbank (Telecom)
7. Muzuho (Banking)
8. Nissan (Automotive)
9. Mitsubishi (Trading Company)
10. Hitachi (Electronics)

more than $62 million to Japan while importing more than $131 million in merchandise. That places the U.S. at a $68 million trade deficit with Japan, which is not unreasonable considering the difference in the size the two nation's populations.

Comparatively, the U.S. exported only $116 million of products to China while importing more than $480 million worth of merchandise in 2015; this created a trade deficit with China exceeding $365 million (**www.census.gov**).

One of the more interesting developments since the attack on Pearl Harbor is the Japanese (and Asian) immigration to Hawaii. The overall Asian population (more than 41 percent) in Hawaii far exceeds the Caucasian population (24 percent), with the Japanese citizens of Hawaii making up more than 16 percent of the state. This is not that surprising when you consider that Japanese were some of the first visitors to the islands and began migrating there long before Hawaii became a U.S. state.

The Pearl Harbor memorial with submarine USS Bowfin in the background.

CONCLUSION

More than 1.8 million visitors from around the world travel to see the *USS Arizona* Memorial as well as the Pearl Harbor Visitor Center each year. The memorial is built over the remains of the sunken battleship where 1,177 crewmen died on December 7, 1941.

People visit the site to experience and honor history, but also to remember the past. Pearl Harbor and the 9/11 attacks have a lot in common. While the situations are different in some ways, both events led to war and changes in people's prejudices. Also, both events impacted the lives of U.S. citizens with similar backgrounds to those who committed the attacks.

Pearl Harbor and the events that followed are merely history stories for most of us. There are few people alive today who can remember any of it first-hand.

In 2014, Joe Langdell and John Anderson were two of nine remaining survivors from the *USS Arizona*. The following year, Langdell died at age 100, and his shipmate, Anderson, died at 98. It was important to them that people remember that the 1,177 men who died on the *Arizona* did not die in vain (McKinnon 2015).

Donald Stratton was also a survivor of the *USS Arizona*. He was interviewed by *People* magazine in 2014. At 92, he recalled that he was just a kid when he served at Pearl Harbor. Even after all those years, Stratton still remembered the sounds of the explosions, the searing heat, and the machine gun blasts from that day. He also remembered the screams of his friends.

"Never a day goes by for all these many years when I haven't thought about it," Stratton said. "I don't talk about it too much, but when December rolls around, I do. It's important the American people don't forget" (Dodd 2014).

We never should forget. Hopefully, we never will.

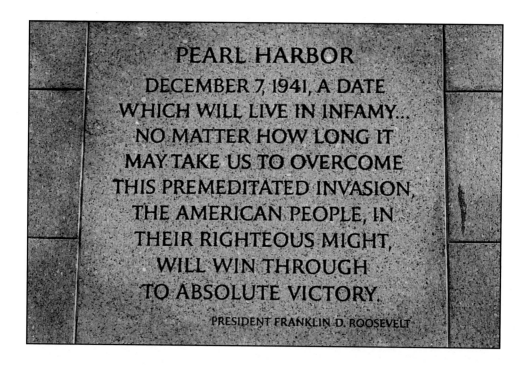

PEARL HARBOR
DECEMBER 7, 1941, A DATE
WHICH WILL LIVE IN INFAMY...
NO MATTER HOW LONG IT
MAY TAKE US TO OVERCOME
THIS PREMEDITATED INVASION,
THE AMERICAN PEOPLE, IN
THEIR RIGHTEOUS MIGHT,
WILL WIN THROUGH
TO ABSOLUTE VICTORY.

PRESIDENT FRANKLIN D. ROOSEVELT

TO THE MEMORY OF THE GALLANT MEN
HERE ENTOMBED AND THEIR SHIPMATES
WHO GAVE THEIR LIVES IN ACTION
ON DECEMBER 7, 1941 ON THE U.S.S. ARIZONA

KEEPING AMERICA STRONG: A PEARL HARBOR SURVIVOR TELLS HIS STORY

Lieutenant Jim Downing is 103, making him the second oldest Pearl Harbor survivor. The Navy sailor served for 24 years from 1932-1956 and was stationed on the *USS West Virginia*.

He's seen a lot in those 103 years of life — horrors, hope, and hardships, but none of that has lessoned the patriotism or vigor of this American gem.

Jim at his home in Colorado Springs

Our editorial team sits down in our warm Florida conference room, notepad and pen in one hand, iPhone on speaker in the other. We introduce ourselves and wish Lt. Downing a happy birthday. He just turned 103 years old on August 22. He laughs and says, "Yes, number one-o-three," as if he's been keeping a tally going to keep track.

Regarding that dreadfully historic day of December 7, 1941, Downing believes the experience provided him and future generations with important obligations. "Well that's just a part of my life," he says. "I enjoyed yesterday, I'm gonna enjoy today, I'm gonna enjoy tomorrow."

On the West Virginia, Downing and the rest of his shipmates were pummeled by nine Japanese torpedoes. Downing was also shot at with machine guns from a plane that flew over.

"One hundred and five men were killed in the attack on my ship," Downing says. "The main damage was done in the first 11 minutes."

After a reprieve in the aerial assault, Downing went into rescue mode. "I got aboard the ship after, and all that was left to do was to take care of the wounded and to try to fight the fire."

The West Virginia was stationed next to the *USS Tennessee*, which was undamaged. Downing, wanting to avoid another explosion if his ship's ammunition caught on fire, grabbed one of the Tennessee's fire hoses.

"As I had the fire hose in one hand, I saw bodies lying around, and one was a friend of mine lying on his back," Downing remembers. "So I tried to turn him over, and then I discovered that the back of his head was blown off."

That painful image didn't steal Downing's eyes for long. He noticed his friend's identification tag and remembered that all of the fallen could be identified this way. Downing was the postmaster on the West Virginia and had access to all of the crew's addresses.

"Their parents would never know what had happened to them, so I resolved to write letters."

Lt. Downing circa 1934

Downing explains that the standard military letters of death notification didn't go into much detail as to how servicemen died, no matter how heroic. He spent the rest of the morning fighting flames and memorizing the names of the fallen.

The nearby *USS Arizona* and the rest of the battleships carried about a million gallons of crude oil that had spilled into the harbor. Downing said the blaze spread to about 200 feet. Even the ocean was on fire.

"I saw sailors who had been blown off their ships submerge and then surface with a film of oil on their bodies. They became human torches and could do nothing about it," he says, admitting this was the saddest sight of that fateful day. "You'd think once they got off the ship in the water they were safe, but if they landed where the oil was on fire, they burned to death."

Some of them were rescued, but many were in areas of such intense heat that rescue boats couldn't get close enough. That afternoon, Downing visited friends and fellow sailors in the hospital, with the intent of writing more letters. Downing spent roughly two hours going down the line, writing down what they said and later transcribing his notes on his manual typewriter.

"They probably couldn't have read my handwriting," Downing laughs.

The content of the letters to families was dictated from the wounded sailors themselves, and most of it came as a bit of a shock to Downing.

"I was kinda surprised at the messages that they sent their parents," Downing says. "Most of them said, 'Don't worry, I'm fine, I'll get well, I'll see ya again.' They never made a complaint, but most of them died that night."

His position as postmaster not only made him popular on payday, it also made him a lifeline of communication in an age when even telephone calls were a luxury. Everything that Downing wrote had to be censored, and he had to be careful not to reveal American intent to fight back or any clue of their location.

"Men in combat have a very fine sense of when there's real danger," Downing says. "When there's no real danger, their behavior is very unusual." Downing explains that he encountered many characters on a ship he described as "a little city," considering that it was two football fields long and could accommodate 1,500 men.

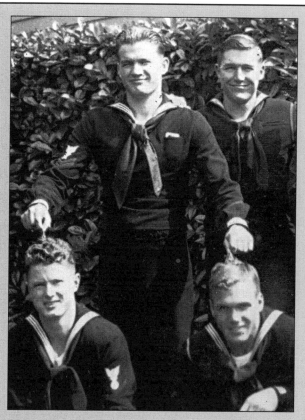

Lt. Jim Downing being a "goofball" according to a close friend of his — he's pictured here pulling the hair of his fellow sailors.

"During a lull in battle, my friend came up and told me he got blown over the side and was saying a prayer." Downing's friend said, "I asked God to give me enough breath to get ashore." And he did — he made it to the other side alive. He continued, "I knew my shortness of breath was due to those cigarettes I was smoking, so I prayed: If you just give me enough breath to get to shore, I'll never smoke again."

Downing says he noticed something while listening to the sailor's story. "I looked down at his arm and I said, 'What's that between your fingers?'"

It was a lighted cigarette. Downing says, "His vow didn't last very long."

Downing was surprised that humor could be shared in the midst of battle, but he also understood its necessity for keeping sane.

As hard as it may be to imagine the range of emotions one may experience in battle, Downing details three.

"The first thing I went through was surprise. There wasn't radar or satellites. We didn't know the Japanese were coming till we saw them. The next thing was fear. The first Japanese plane I saw shot at me with machine guns. Fortunately, he didn't hit me. The third thing was anger — that our political and military leadership had let this happen. I made a resolve that if I ever was in a position of authority that we'd never get caught that way again."

It's easy to tell in his voice, however, that the fourth emotion he felt that day has carried him well for the last 75 years.

"The final thing was pride," he says. "Everyone did the right thing, regardless of the cost of their lives. I was really proud the way people reacted and did the impossible."

In a message to the current generation, Downing is blunt but no less caring in tone.

"Whether you like it or not, your generation will be the leaders in America," Downing says. "You will be the voters in America. You will be the taxpayers in America."

Downing also offers a phrase worthy of the heroism displayed on that day of infamy and an arguably invaluable philosophy.

"Weakness invites aggression," he says. "Keep America strong. I want to see America so strong that no tyrant, or no government of a tyrant, will ever attack us. That means keeping strong in cyberspace, in the skies, on the ground, in the sea, and under the sea."

The interview is coming to a close, and like most journalists, we ask Jim one final question: "Is there anything else you want to say?"

He responds, "I have discovered two main things. The first is that the Japanese made not one, but they made eight attacks on Pacific and Asian targets within a 24-hour period. And I just emphasize the other: Weakness invites aggression. Keep America strong."

We close the interview and part ways, and as our editorial staff sits on the edge of our cushy seats, there is a silent presence in the air — a presence of awe, of wonder, and of profound reverence. Moments pass as we all experience this feeling, and then the hustle and bustle begins again: keyboards clicking, mouses scrolling, recordings playing, and emails pinging. In this hectic world we live in, it's worthwhile to sit back and recall what America was like when a man — a hero — risked his life to protect our country.

And as we press on, I encourage all of us to sit back for a moment and let Lt. Jim Downing's final words resonate in us: Weakness invites aggression. Keep America strong.

Lt. Jim Downing, at 103 years old, is sitting next to a picture of his 21-year-old self. The star on his arm means that he is an "Unrestricted Line Officer." Unrestricted Line Officers are qualified to command at sea the Navy's warfighting combatant units such as warships, submarines, aviation squadrons, and SEAL teams.

EVENT TIMELINES

The chapters of this book detail out many of the events leading up to and following Pearl Harbor. However, there are many more events related to World War II that the pages of this book could not cover. To provide a more complete glimpse at the Second World War and how the attack on Pearl Harbor fit into it, three separate timelines have been provided here.

The first timeline is an overview of events that led up to the start of World War II. Since many historians believe that the results of WWI had a direct impact on the WWII, the timeline begins there and covers events around the globe that may have led to Japan, Germany, and Italy going to war.

The second and third timelines provide an overview of the war in both Europe and the Pacific. Naturally, the attack on Pearl Harbor led to war with Japan and the ensuring conflict in the Pacific, but it was also the chief reason the U.S. entered the war in Europe. As a result, the events that follow on both fronts were a direct result of the Japanese attack on December 7th, 1941.

Overview of Events Prior to WWII

- Late 1918 marks the end of World War I. The German Kaiser Wilhilm II abandons the throne and flees to the Netherlands; Germany is declared a Republic.

- In the later months of 1918, an armistice goes into effect that requires German submarines to be imprisoned by the Allies and all major German warships to be disarmed.

- In early 1919, the draft of the "Covenant" of the League of Nations is completed. A few months later, the Treaty of Versailles is submitted to the German delegation. The treaty is signed in late June of 1919, officially ending the war. It contained strong reparation requirements that amounted to billions of dollars.

- With a growing sense of Isolationism, the U.S. does not sign the Versailles Treaty and opts out of the League of Nations. The U.S. makes a separate and equally harsh treaty with Germany and the Axis powers.

- In 1920, Russia and Poland go to war; the League of Nations grants Britain the right to rule over Iraq, resulting in an Iraqi revolt.

- In 1921, Adolf Hitler becomes the head of the Nazi Party in Germany.

- Throughout 1921 and 1922, the Washington Naval Conference meets with the goal of promoting peace. During this time, multiple nations sign the Five-Power

Treaty, the Four-Power Treaty, and the Nine-Power Treaty. These treaties are designed to promote disarmament and to discourage conflict between Japan and China.

- In late 1922, Mussolini is invited by King Victor Emmanuel III to form a coalition Government in Italy; Mussolini gradually turns Italy into a fascist dictatorship.

- The U.S. passes the Immigration Act of 1924, limiting the number of immigrants allowed into America through a national origins quota. The legislation completely eliminates immigration from Asian nations.

- In 1924, the Dawes Plan lowers Germany's annual reparation payments, increasing them over time as the country's economy improves. U.S. financier JP Morgan floats a loan on the U.S. market, and other U.S. banks lend Germany enough money to enable it to meet its reparation payments to France and the UK.

- Germany is admitted into the League of Nations in 1926.

- In April of 1926, the Treaty of Berlin is signed by Germany and the Soviet Union, which declares neutrality if either country is attacked within the next five years.

- In early 1929, the amount of reparations demanded of Germany decreases and is set to be paid over a 58-year period. Another loan would be floated in foreign markets.

- The Wall Street Stock Market crashes in late 1929, starting the Great Depression, which is felt not just in the U.S., but also worldwide.

- Japanese expansion into Manchuria advances in late 1931.

- Hitler is elected Chancellor of Germany in January of 1933. In March of 1933, the Enabling Act is passed, which makes Hitler the dictator of Germany.

- In March of 1933, Japan leaves the League of Nations. Later in October of that same year, Germany exits the League.

- In April of 1933, the Gestapo secret police is established. A few months later, all non-Nazi parties are banned in Germany.

- In October of 1933, scientist Albert Einstein arrives in the U.S. as a refuge from Germany.

- In 1933, Germany begins sending people to concentration camps.

- Mexico seizes foreign-owned oil properties in 1933, and Britain breaks relations with them; however, Roosevelt maintains U.S. relations and establishes a "good neighbor" policy.

- In January of 1934, Germany and Poland sign a 10-year German-Polish Non-Aggression Pact.

- In July of 1934, Austrian Chancellor Dollfuss is killed during a Nazi uprising.

- In December of 1934, Japan renounces the Washington Naval Treaty, singling their intension to strengthen their navy and advance their territory in Asia.

- In June of 1935, the Anglo-German Naval Agreement is signed between Germany and the UK; the pact allows Germany to build a fleet that was 35 percent the tonnage of the British fleet. In this way, the UK hopes to keep German naval re-armament in check.

- The U.S. Congress passes the first Neutrality Act in August of 1935, prohibiting the export of arms, ammunition, and implements of war from the U.S. to foreign nations at war. In February of 1936, Congress renews the Act and prohibits Americans from extending loans to belligerent nations.

- In March of 1936, Germany violates the Treaty of Versailles and remilitarizes the Rhineland that had been occupied by France.

- In May of 1936, Mussolini's army conquers Ethiopia. The League of Nations condemns Italy for that action, and Mussolini begins to switch his loyalties to Germany and Hitler.

- Civil War erupts in Spain in 1936.

- In November of 1936, Germany and Japan agree to the Anti-Comintern Pact. Both parties agree to go to war with the Soviet Union if the other party is attacked.

- With the passage of the Neutrality Act of 1937, U.S. citizens are forbidden from traveling on belligerent ships, and American merchant ships are prevented from transporting arms to those nations. Ships from belligerent nations could be barred from U.S. waters, and the president was authorized to place embargos on any other "articles or materials."

- The conflict between Japan and China begins on the Marco Polo Bridge near Peking in July of 1937.

- In November of 1937, Italy joins the Anti-Comintern Pact with Germany and Japan. In December, Italy leaves the League of Nations.

- In March of 1938, Austria is incorporated by Germany, and Japanese troops reach the Yellow River in China.

- In the summer of 1938, the Soviet Union and Japan engage in border conflict that begins at the Battle of Khasan (in which the Soviets win).

- In September of 1938, the Munich Agreement is signed by Germany, France, the UK, and Italy, allowing Germany to annex the Czechoslovak Sudetenland area in exchange for peace.

- In January of 1939, Hitler launches a five-year naval expansion program known as Plan Z.

- In the spring of 1939, Germany violates the Munich Agreement and occupies the Czech territory not previously granted for annexation. Germany also demands that the Klaipeda Region (former parts of Germany once known as East Prussia) and the Free City of Danzig return to German control.

- In April of 1939, Italy invades Albania.

- In May of 1939, the Pact of Steel is signed between Italy and Germany, declaring cooperation and a military alliance between the two powers.

- In June of 1939, the Japanese blockade the British concession in the North China Treaty Port of Tientsin.

- In September of 1939, Germany invades Poland, officially starting World War II in Europe.

- The U.S. Congress passes the Neutrality Act of 1939 in November despite President Roosevelt's efforts to involve the country on the side of the Allies in what was now World War II.

- In 1940, President Roosevelt persuades the U.S. Congress to accept a Lend-Lease agreement that would allow the U.S. to "lend" supplies to countries such as Britain with them deferring payment. When payment is made, it would be made in terms of considerations once the war was complete. The U.S. extends billions of dollars in assistance under this agreement, bypassing the previously passed Neutrality Acts.

- The Tripartite Pact, or Berlin Pact, is signed in September of 1940. It's an agreement between Germany, Italy, and Japan that is later joined by Hungary, Romania, Bulgaria, Yugoslavia, and Slovakia. It's essentially the formation of the Axis powers of WWII.

- On December 7th, 1941, Japan bombs Pearl Harbor and declares war on the U.S., bringing America into WWII.

Overview of the War in Europe

- In September of 1939, Germany invades Poland, officially starting World War II in Europe. In response, Britain, France, Australia, Canada, and New Zealand declare war on Germany.

- The U.S. passes its final Neutrality Act, remaining out of the war for the time being.

- In response to the Germany invasion of Poland, the Soviets also invade. The Nazis and the Soviets divide the country.

- In November of 1939, the Soviets attack Finland and are expelled from the League of Nations the following month.

- In March of 1940, Finland signs a peace treaty with the Soviets, and Germans bomb a naval base near Scotland.

- In April and May of 1940, the Nazis invade Denmark, Norway, France, Belgium, Luxembourg, and the Netherlands. Denmark, Holland, and Belgium surrender.

- In June of 1940, Germany bombs Paris, and Norway surrenders. Italy declares war on Britain and France while Germany marches into Paris. France signs an armistice with the Nazis.

- Also in June of 1940, the Soviets begin occupation of the Baltic States.

- In July of 1940, the Battle of Britain begins, and the Soviets take Lithuania, Latvia, and Estonia.

- In August of 1940, Italy occupies British Somaliland in East Africa and air raids/battles take place over Britain. Hitler also orchestrates a blockage of the British Isles.

- In August of 1940, the British strike back with air raids on Berlin.

- In September of 1940, Germany continues to attack Britain; Italy invades Egypt.

- The Tripartite (Axis) Pact is signed by Germany, Italy, and Japan in September of 1940.

- In October of 1940, Germany invades Romania while Italy invades Greece.

- In November of 1940, Hungary and Romania join the Axis Powers.

- In December of 1940, the British begin a western desert offensive in North Africa against Italy. By January of 1941, the British and Australians and winning ground in Africa.

- In early 1941, German forces arrive in North Africa while British forces join Greece.

- By April of 1941, Nazis invade Yugoslavia and Greece; each country surrenders.

- In May of 1941, the heavy German bombing of London begins.

- In June of 1941, the Allies invade Syria and Lebanon; Germany attacks the Soviet Union.

- In July of 1941, a Mutual Assistance agreement is formed between Britain and the Soviets.

- In August of 1941, the Nazi siege of Leningrad begins.

- In September of 1941, Nazis take Kiev.

- In October of 1941, the Germans begin an advance on Moscow and take Odesa.

- In December of 1941, the Soviet Army launches a major counter-offensive, and the Japanese attack Pearl Harbor. The U.S. and Britain declare war on Japan; Germany declares war on the U.S.; America enters the war on the side of the Allies.

- In January of 1942, Germany begins a U-boat offensive along the East Coast of the U.S. The first American forces arrive in Great Britain.

- In the summer of 1942, Germans besiege Sevastopol. Rommel captures Tobruk and reaches El Alamein near Cairo, Egypt. The Germans also began a drive toward Stalingrad.

- By September of 1942, Rommel is driven back by Montgomery and has withdrawn from El Agheila by December. At the same time, the Soviets defeat Italian troops on the River Don in the USSR.

- In January of 1943, Germany begins to withdraw from the Caucasus, and the Soviets begin an offensive against the Germans in Stalingrad.

- In February of 1943, Germany surrenders at Stalingrad, and Soviets begin retaking territory.

- In March of 1943, Germany withdraws from Tunisia, Africa; Montgomery's Eighth Army breaks the enemy lines weeks later. In May, the Allies take Tunisia, and both German and Italian troops surrender in North Africa.

- In July of 1943, Allied forces land in Sicily and begin bombing Rome. The Americans capture Palermo, Sicily; Mussolini is arrested, triggering the fall of the Italian Fascist government. By September, Italy has officially surrendered to the Allies.

- In October of 1943, Italy declares war on Germany.

- In November of 1943, Russians recapture Kiev in Ukraine, and Britain launches large air raids on Berlin.

- By January of 1944, Soviet troops advance into Poland.

- In May of 1944, Germans surrender in the Crimea and retreat from Anzio.

- In June of 1944, D-Day landings commence on the northern coast of France, and U.S. troops liberate Cherbourg, France within weeks. In the months that followed, British, U.S., and Canadian troops liberated much of France.

- In the summer of 1944, the Soviets launch a major offensive and liberate the first concentration camp at Majdanek. By August, the Soviets advance into Romania.

- In September of 1944, Finland and the Soviet Union agree to a cease-fire; U.S. troops reach the Siegfried Line in Western Germany.

- In October of 1944, the Allies liberate Athens, and a massive German surrender occurrs at Aachen, Germany.

- In November of 1944, French troops reach the Rhine and capture Strasbourg.

- In December of 1944, the Battle of the Bulge takes place between U.S. and Germany; the Soviet troops besiege Budapest.

- In January of 1945, Germans withdraw from the Ardennes; Soviet troops capture Warsaw, Poland and liberate Auschwitz.

- In March of 1945, the Allies take Cologne and establish a bridge across the Rhine. Soviet troops capture Danzig.

- In April of 1945, the Allies liberate Buchenwald and Belsen concentration camps. The Soviets begin their attack on

Berlin, and the Americans enter Nuremberg. The U.S. 7th Army liberates Dachau; Adolf Hitler commits suicide.

- In May of 1945, Germany unconditionally surrenders to the Allies. May 8th is known as VE (Victory in Europe) Day.

Overview of the War in the Pacific

- The conflict between Japan and China begins on the Marco Polo Bridge near Peking in July of 1937. For the purpose of the War in the Pacific, this is the start of WWII.

- By December of 1937, Japan establishes the puppet state of Mengjian in the Inner Mongolia region of the Republic of China.

- In the summer of 1938, border conflicts erupt between the Soviets and the Japanese leading to the Battle of Lake Khasan.

- In late 1938, Roosevelt asks Congress for $500 million to increase America's defense forces. The Japanese see the buildup of the U.S. military as a direct threat to their empire.

- In February of 1939, Japan occupies Hainan Island on the southern coast of China, improving their ability to ban naval trade routes.

- In May of 1939, The Battle of Khalkhin Gol is fought between Japan and the Soviet Union; the Soviets were victorious. This leads Japan to not seek further conflict with the Soviets, but to turn toward Pacific holdings of the Euro-American powers instead.

- In June of 1939, the Japanese blockade the British concession in the North China Treaty Port of Tientsin.

- In July of 1940, trade sanctions are imposed on Japan, creating additional tensions between them and the U.S.

- In September of 1940, Japan signs the Tripartite Pact (or Berlin Pact) with Germany and Italy forming a defensive military alliance.

- By January of 1941, Admiral Yamamoto communicates with other Japanese officers to formalize a plan to attack Pearl Harbor.

- In April of 1941, American scientists develop a machine to break the code on Japanese secret diplomatic messages. Intelligence is gathered that indicates a potential attack, but officials in Washington continue to believe it would be somewhere other than Pearl Harbor.

- In July of 1941, Roosevelt freezes Japanese assets in the U.S. and suspends relations.

- In August of 1941, the U.S. announces an oil embargo against aggressor states, including Japan.

- On November 26, 1941, Japan aircraft carriers and escorts depart from Japanese waters.

- On December 7th, 1941 the Japanese bomb Pearl Harbor, also attacking the Philippines, Guam, Thailand, Shanghai, and Midway. Within days, the U.S., Britain, and China declare war on Japan.

- Later in December of 1941, the Japanese invade British Borneo, Hong Kong, and the Philippines. General Douglas MacArthur withdraws from Manila to Bataan. Also, Japan bombs Manila.

- In January of 1942, the Japanese attack at Bataan in the Philippines, invade the Dutch East Indies, and begin advancement in Burma.

- The German, Japanese, and Italian military agreement is signed in Berlin in January of 1942.

- In late January of 1942, a U.S. sub sinks the first Japanese warship. By February, the first U.S. aircraft carrier offensive of the war is launched as the *USS Yorktown*; *USS Enterprise* conducts air raids on Japanese bases in Gilbert and Marshall islands.

- In February of 1942, Japan invades Singapore and Sumatra. They also launch an air raid against Australia and invade Bali.

- On February 23, 1942, a Japanese submarine shells an oil refinery near Santa Barbara, CA; the *USS Enterprise* attacks the Japanese on Wake Island, but in the Battle of the Java Sea, the *USS Houston* is sunk.

- In March of 1942, two Japanese flying boats bomb Pearl Harbor, but they give away their refueling location, and the *USS Enterprise* attacks Marcus Island, just 1,000 miles from Japan.

- In March of 1942, the British evacuate Burma, and the Dutch surrender Java to Japan; the Japanese also invade Salamaua and Lea on New Guinea.

- In April of 1942, the U.S. starts relocating Japanese-Americans to relocation centers and internment camps.

- In April of 1942, U.S. troops arrive in Australia, but U.S. forces on Bataan surrender to the Japanese. The Bataan Death March begins on April 10, 1942 as 76,000 Allied POWs were forced to walk 60 miles without food or water to a new camp; 5,000 of the 12,000 U.S. POWs died during the march.

- In May of 1942, Japan takes central Burma, Tulagi in the Solomon Islands and prepares to invade Midway and the Aleutian Islands. U.S. and Filipino forces surrender in the Philippines, but Japan suffers its first defeat during the Battle of the Coral Sea.

- In June of 1942, the U.S. wins the Battle of Midway, destroying four Japanese carriers and a cruiser while damaging another cruiser and two destroyers. The U.S. only loses the *USS Yorktown* during that fight.

- In August of 1942, U.S. Marines take the unfinished airfield on Guadalcanal. However, the same day, the U.S.

suffers a huge naval defeat when eight Japanese warships wage a night attack and sink four U.S. ships and one Australian cruiser in less than an hour.

- In September of 1942, a Japanese floatplane drops incendiary bombs on U.S. forests in Oregon. Newspapers in the U.S. voluntarily withhold that information.

- Also in September of 1942, the Battle of the Bloody Ridge is fought on Guadalcanal, and the British go on the offensive in Burma.

- In October of 1942, the Battle of Santa Cruz of Guadalcanal takes place.

- In November of 1942, the Japanese conduct air raids in Darwin, Australia.

- In December of 1942, Emperor Hirohito gives permission to Japanese troops to withdraw from Guadalcanal. Evacuation begins in February of 1943.

- In April of 1943, U.S. code breakers pinpoint the location of Japanese Admiral Yamamoto, and the U.S. sends 18 P-38 fighters to shoot him down.

- In May of 1943, U.S. troops invade Attu in the Aleutian Islands; later that month, the Japanese end the occupation of the islands.

- In June of 1943, Allies advance to New Georgia, Solomon Islands and complete the occupation by August.

- In November of 1943, U.S. troops invade Makin and Tarawa in the Gilbert Islands, and shortly thereafter, the Japanese withdraw.

- In January of 1944, British and Indian troops recapture Maungdaw in Burma.

- In February of 1944, U.S. troops capture Kwajalein and Majura Atolls in the Marshall Islands. U.S. carrier-based planes destroy the Japanese naval base at Truk in the Caroline Islands, the base at Rabaul, and facilities at the Mariana Islands.

- In April of 1944, Japan begins its last offensive in China, attacking U.S. air bases located in Eastern China. Meanwhile, Allied forces invade multiple locations in New Guinea.

- In June of 1944, 47 B-29s based in India bomb steel works in Yawata, Japan.

- In late summer and fall of 1944, American troops liberate Guam. U.S. and Chinese troops take Myitkyina; the U.S. completes the capture of the Mariana Islands.

- In October of 1944, the U.S. begins air raids against Okinawa. That same month, the first Kamikaze (or suicide air) attacks occurr against the U.S. warships in Leyte Gulf, though the battle is still a decisive victory for the U.S. Navy.

- In November of 1944, B-29s bomb the Nakajima aircraft facility near Tokyo.

- In February of 1945, U.S. troops recapture Bataan in the Philippines while U.S. Marines invade Iowa Jima.

- In March of 1945, the U.S. fire bombs Tokyo.

- In April of 1945, the U.S. Tenth Army invades Okinawa.

- May 8th, 1945 is Victory Day in Europe. Weeks later, Japan begins to withdraw from China.

- In June of 1945, the Japanese make it clear that they will not accept unconditional surrender. However, resistance ends in Okinawa as the U.S. Tenth Army completes its capture.

- In July of 1945, the Philippines are fully liberated, and 1,000 bomber raids begin against Japan. That same month, the first Atomic bomb is tested in the U.S.

- August of 1945, the U.S. drops two atomic bombs on Hiroshima and Nagasaki, pushing the Japanese into unconditional surrender. Shortly, U.S. troops land near Tokyo to begin occupation of Japan, and the British reoccupy Hong Kong.

- September 2, 1945 is known as VJ (Victory over Japan) Day.

GLOSSARY

American Isolationism: A doctrine that a nation should stay out of the disputes and affairs of other nations. The U.S. practiced a policy of isolationism until World War I and revisited the policy after that until the bombing of Pearl Harbor.

Bolshevik Revolution: Otherwise known as the Russian Revolution, this refers to the overthrow of the Tsars in Russia and then the removal of the provincial government and the rise of the Bolsheviks, or the communist party, in Russia.

Capitalism: An economic and political system where a country's trade and industry are controlled by private owners rather than by the state.

Communism: A political theory derived from Karl Marx that advocates an economic system where all property is publicly owned and each person works and is paid according to their abilities and needs; there is no privately owned property under this system.

Fascism: An authoritarian and nationalistic system of government where the state controls commerce and the lives of the people and limits the individual rights of the people.

Gross Domestic Product (GDP): A monetary value of all the finished goods and services produced within a country's borders in a specific time period. GDP is usually calculated on an annual basis and includes all private and public consumption, government outlays, investments, and exports (minus. imports) that occur within a nation (or other defined region).

Industrialization: The process in which a society or country transforms itself from primarily agricultural-based income into one based on the manufacturing of goods.

Nazism: Similar to fascism, it is an authoritarian hierarchical government and economic system based on state ownership of capital.

Nisei: The child of Japanese immigrants who was born and educated in the Americas, specifically in the U.S. (Japanese-born immigrants are referred to as Issei).

Martial Law: A law temporarily imposed upon an area by state or national military forces in replacement of civil authority when government has broken down or during wartime military operations. Also, law imposed on a defeated country or occupied territory by the military forces of the occupying power.

McCarthyism: A movement named after Senator Joseph McCarthy who rose to national prominence by initiating a probe to identify U.S. citizens who were members or were sympathetic to the communist party. The hunt for communists in America led to the formation of the House Committee on Un-American Activities and the process of "blacklisting" individuals who were suspected, but not proven, of treacherous actions.

Trade Deficit: A trade deficit occurs when the value of a country's imports exceeds the value of its exports. This scenario represents an outflow of domestic currency to foreign markets.

BIBLIOGRAPHY

Andrews, Evan. "8 Things You May Not Know About the Battle of the Bulge." **http://History.com**. A&E Television Networks, 16 Dec. 2014. Web. 20 Apr. 2016.

Donohue, Nathan, "Understanding the Decision to Drop the Bomb on Hiroshima and Nagasaki," Center for Strategic & International Studies, **http://csis.org**, 2012.

Dodd, Johnny, "One of the Last Living Pearl Harbor Survivors Remembers 'Painful' Day," *People,* **www.people.com**, 2014.

"First Transit: 100 Years of the U.S. Navy in the Panama Canal," **www.navalhistory.org**, 2014.

Fischer, John, "A Brief History of Pearl Harbor Prior to World War II, Origins of Pearl Harbor," **http://gohawaii.about.com**, 2015.

"General William 'Billy' Mitchell and the Sinking of the Ostfriesland: A Consideration," The National Air and Space Museum, **http://blog.nasm.si.edu**, 2011.

Higgs, Robert, "How U.S. Economic Warfare Provoked Japan's Attack on Pearl Harbor," Independent Institute, **www.independent.org**, 2006.

"The History of Pearl Harbor," **www.nps.gov**, 2016.

Horne, Alistair, "Payback for Pearl," **www.historynet.com**, 2012.

Holley, Peter, "With their numbers shrinking, Pearl Harbor survivors make final pilgrimages to Hawaii," **www. washingtonpost.com**, 2014.

Interesting-Facts.com. "Pearl Harbor Facts — 10 Facts about Pearl Harbor Attack." *Interesting Facts*. 17 Feb. 2015. Web. 20 Apr. 2016.

Jones, Steve, "The United States and Japan After World War II, From Enemies to Allies," **http://usforeignpolicy.about. com,** 2014.

Kennedy, Rita, "Japanese Imperialism During the 1930s," **http://classroom.synonym.com**, 2016.

McAvoy, Audrey, "Pearl Harbor survivors share stories of attack," **www.seattletimes.com**, 2011.

McKillop, Jack, "United State Navy Aircraft Carriers, December 7, 1941," **http://bluejacket.com**, 2016.

McKinnon, Shaun, "USS Arizona's Oldest Survivor dies at 100," *The Arizona Republic,* **www.azcentral.com**, 2015.

McKinnon, Shaun, "John Anderson, one of the last USS Arizona survivors, dies at 98," *The Arizona Republic,* **www.azcentral. com**, 2015.

Melinger, Philip, *The Paths of Heaven: The Evolution of Air Power Theory,* Air University Press, Alabama, 1997.

Nordyke, Eleanor C. and Matsumoto, Y. Scott, "The Japanese in Hawaii: a historical and demographic perspective," **http://evols.library.manoa.hawaii.edu**, 1977.

Perloff, James, "Pearl Harbor: Hawaii Was Surprised; FDR Was Not," **www.thenewamerican.com**, 2015.

Placide, Krislyn, "The Secret Weapons Behind the Japanese Attack on Pearl Harbor," **www.popsci.com**, 2012.

"Remembering Pearl Harbor: A Pearl Harbor Fact Sheet," **http://nationalww2mU.S.eum.org**, 2016.

Riley, Charles, "Japan now holds more U.S. debt than China," **http://money.cnn.com**, 2015.

Toland, John. *Infamy: Pearl Harbor and Its Aftermath,* Doubleday & Company, Inc., Garden City, NY, 1982.

Trueman, C.N., "Pearl Harbor 1941" **www.historylearningsite.co.uk**. 2015.

Weintraub, Stanley, *Long Day's Journey into War, December 7th, 1941,* Truman Talley Books, New York, 1991.

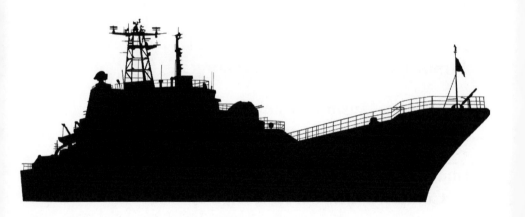

INDEX

ABOUT THE AUTHOR

Kimberly Sarmiento is a writer, researcher, and educator who developed and delivered undergraduate courses such as *American Federal Government* and *Political Parties and Interest Groups* at Cameron University.

Ms. Sarmiento is a graduate from the University of Florida with a Masters in Political Science and a Bachelors in Journalism. Over the course of her career, she has written for three regional newspapers, authored two books and several blogs on career management, and worked on customized development of marketing material that ranges from Web content to resumes.

Recently, Ms. Sarmiento has been engaged on a volunteer basis to provide advice to teens on how they can translate high school experience into résumé content for the job market or for college admissions. In her spare time, she enjoys reading and going to theme parks with her children.